I'VE GOT YOUR BACK

The Essential Guide to Marketing Your Therapy Business

HELEN BULLEN

R3THINK PRESS

First published in Great Britain in 2019
by Rethink Press (www.rethinkpress.com)

Cover image © Shutterstock | ace03

Contents

Foreword

So, you've studied hard and qualified as a professional therapist, and now you are in your therapy practice. Maybe you've been out in practice for a few years; either way, is there an 'elephant in your therapy room' – one that says, 'Am I really going to get all those clients and make a success of my business?' Or worse still, 'I've been doing this for a while and still am not seeing those high numbers of clients I was promised. Why not?'

Look around and you'll soon find a 'business expert' who will be eager to suggest you follow their 'three- / five- / nine-step plan' to become financially secure like them. Do you ever ask yourself, if they are so financially secure why do they need you to pay them to follow their plan? I've often pondered this question myself. Well, a common denominator in most of their 'plans' involves implementing an external 'one size fits all' strategy, and then hey presto, according to the 'experts', the clients will appear... Yeah right, and I believe in the Tooth Fairy too!

This book is different for two significant reasons. Firstly, Helen does not bombard you with a series of generic steps to follow, nor does she ram her own brand of 'snake oil' at you, insisting that you must buy it to become successful in your own right.

What Helen does is pose thought-provoking questions and provide examples (which I'm sure many of you will recognise and have experienced) from her own personal journey to establishing her highly successful, multi-award-winning therapy business. The book enables you to more fully explore and understand your personal and individual journey as a practitioner.

But Helen doesn't stop there. The second reason why this book is different to others promising that 'pot of gold' is evident from the first page. The content of the book and her writing style deals in a passionate and compassionate way with the real issues which all therapists will have faced at some point in their professional careers. However, in true 'Helen style', she doesn't pull any punches, so don't expect to come away from reading this book without facing a few home truths. But doesn't that just make the final achievement all the sweeter?

Throughout the book Helen sets you challenges (eg 'Just stop' and 'Time to Brain Dump' are two of my favourites), which not only leave you more insightful about your own self, but if you take nothing more from this book, these will provide you with a range of 'tools'. Used in the right way, these tools just may help you unlock the answers in those not-so-easy times – those times when you especially feel the weight of being a sole practitioner having to deal with issues on your own, as many of us will have done. Don't be fooled though, this book isn't just for those in practice on their own, the sections dealing with customer care, branding and marketing are invaluable for any sized practice wanting to stand out in the overcrowded and highly competitive marketplace.

Helen's practical understanding of marketing strategies and advice on the effective use of social media combined with those challenges make this not only a book to read to gain fundamental knowledge, but also to use a reference guide to dip into if and when the situation warrants it.

In my career as an osteopathic lecturer and programme leader, and as principal of two osteopathic colleges, I have taught over 600 osteopathy students and enabled them to graduate as osteopaths both in the UK and Europe. Helen has stood out as one of the most empathetic and committed students of them all. When Helen became an osteopathic lecturer, her honest and open approach was always one that students valued. She brings this same approach to her writing in this book.

The title of this book says it all, because in helping you to realise your ambitions for your therapy business, you can be sure that Helen has researched the relevant and important areas or personally experienced the issues herself, and proposes some useful solutions you may want to consider. She wants you to achieve, not for her own accolades, but because she really does 'have your back'. I have been a registered osteopath in practice for over thirty years now, but I wish this book and its advice had been available to me many years ago. It certainly would have made my journey much easier.

If you want a get rich quick scheme then this book isn't for you but if, like me and also the many others whom Helen has mentored, you want to become more fulfilled and cognisant with the modern business of being a therapist then do yourself a favour and invest your time in reading this book.

Melanie Coutinho, Registered Osteopath; Director of Programme Development, Accademia per lo Sviluppo dell'Osteopatia e della Medicina Integrativa (ASOMI), Turin, Italy

Introduction

Marketing. That word usually conjures up images of heavy sales which take a ton of work with little return. Is that how you see it?

Marketing is essential to your business, but it doesn't have to be an arduous task that makes you feel sleazy and queasy. If you have had your business for any length of time, it is likely you have heard of a range of marketing methods. So-called experts tell you there is a set system, a quick way to sell or work to see great results. You may believe that you need to 'niche your ideal client' and 'focus on your specific avatar'. You may have been told to get your treatments on to discounted platforms that in reality give you little return. Often you are asked to work out your unique selling point (USP). Social media can seem like a minefield.

It is tempting to look for a magic template which will attract a steady stream of clients. But some marketing methods can feel like you are tricking, even forcing your client into buying from you. Not a nice way to feel. I certainly had to wrestle with my misconceptions on marketing before I started to get results.

Be careful not to fall for sleazy sales techniques that use your desire to get more clients to convince you that you need to spend a lot of money for *the* secret miracle system. The marketing gurus who hype you up into a frenzy so that when they sell, you feel compelled to buy without looking at the effectiveness of what is on offer. Salespeople who exploit your need so they can make quick money for little work. If it seems too good to be true, it probably is.

Quick-fix methods will *not* guarantee you more clients. In fact, quite the opposite. If you make your niche too specific, you can lose a huge part of your ideal audience. Discounted platforms will bring you clients who want something for nothing and won't value your time and skills or return after the offer has finished. Automated sales funnels make your clients stop coming to see you as they feel constantly 'sold to' with email after email.

There is no secret method to make the clients just roll in. Instead, there are methods that work. Methods that will take action from you for the lifetime of your business, both consistently and persistently. I will never promise you false marketing hopes, but I will always help you make things happen.

Of course, some marketing methods are effective, and I will be talking in-depth about how you can use them without feeling sleazy, but if you don't take care of the things that prevent you committing to taking action, then they will be all but useless to you. Instead of getting more clients, you're likely to become disillusioned, fed up and lacking in self-confidence, and ultimately you may think marketing is a waste of time. Worst case scenario, you'll give up on doing the job you love.

There is a huge gap between having a dream and taking effective action to get the results you want. This is obvious in all areas of your life when you wish you could have something; when you wish you could achieve a specific goal. It is likely you start out full of enthusiasm. For a few days, or maybe even weeks, things are positive and you are confident that you can achieve your dream. It looks possible, it looks easy. There is no way you will stop. How hard can it really be? But the reality is you are caught up in the initial dream phase of an idea.

Coaching and mentoring therapists, I realised that despite the fact I was giving people great marketing methods, they were still struggling to take effective action to get the results they wanted. There was something else that was missing.

This made me think long and hard about what I had done to achieve my own goals. What did I do naturally that made me take action, confident that I could achieve anything I wanted? Yes, I had worked hard on increasing my knowledge of marketing methods, but what *exactly* did I do that made those methods more than just a list? What made me take action persistently and consistently? What made me commit to anything I wanted to achieve?

It took one of my business coaches to point out that not everyone worked like me. Over time, I worked out five main principles: a framework that I instinctively used. It shocked me that I had missed this essential piece of the success puzzle and I vowed that my coaching would be different from then on. To help people just like you really reach your potential, I had to shout my five Commit to Achieve principles as loudly as I shouted about marketing methods.

Throughout this book, we will use my key principles as the framework, but the true key to your business success is your commitment. When you learn to commit, you raise your chances of achieving your goals at least tenfold.

My key Commit to Achieve principles are:

1. Care of self
2. Know your why

3. Release limiting beliefs

4. Understand how

5. Take effective action

I will go into more detail throughout the book, but I will outline each principle here so you can immediately see their background and benefits.

Care of self, my number-one principle, is the one that many business owners either ignore or put at the bottom of their list. It can be easy to think that you have to get on and run your business, being too busy being busy to look after yourself. Have you ever thought how important it is for you to stay fit and well not just to have a healthy lifestyle, but also to have a healthy business?

I encourage every business owner I work with to take care of themselves. As soon as you make you your priority, you will feel calmer and more able to deal with stress. Your focus will increase, as will your self-confidence. Care of self helps you become more rational when making decisions. Your concentration will improve and your productivity will increase.

Make care of self your priority. Don't underestimate the power of this important principle.

My second principle is to **know your why**. It is so easy to forget your initial dreams and aspirations for your business. You forget why you started, and then it may feel like your business has not become what you set it out to be in the first place.

For any success, you need to know your why. Why do you do what you do? What do you love about your work? What motivates you to succeed? I want you to let your imagination run wild. Re-energise, motivate and inspire yourself, and commit to building a business that you truly want and enjoy.

Your why is an important motivation and gives you the reason to keep pushing forward on your success journey, taking consistent and persistent action. It is pretty much impossible to gain success without knowing your why, so I'll share how to work it out and set goals and targets to get to your business utopia.

Principle number three is to **release limiting beliefs**. Nearly all the business owners I have worked with have had limiting beliefs that stopped them building the business they really wanted. It's not sales funnels, or Facebook posts, or ability that holds you back; it's your limiting beliefs. Beliefs that you are not good enough; feelings of being an imposter; fear of what others will say; negative beliefs about money – the list goes on and on.

For every struggle we have in our business, there is usually a limiting belief story behind it. We create reasons why we can't take action or move our business forward, but the harsh truth is those reasons are just excuses covering a limiting belief. Excuses are the best way to stay stuck where we are; to never deliver on our dreams; to get frustrated and give up.

Just as we have limiting beliefs about ourselves, we also have limiting beliefs about others. Comparing ourselves to others, we convince ourselves we could never do what they do. We start trying to mind read what they are thinking about us, which can stop us dead in our tracks.

In this book, I will focus on key limiting beliefs and how you can recognise and counteract them. I am not going to tell you this is simple, but with some work and helpful techniques, you *can* overcome the things that are currently holding you back.

To run a business, you need to know how to do it. **Understanding how** is about getting clients, both new and returning, continually rocking up to your door. Knowing which marketing methods to use and when to use them is key to your business survival. Create a community around you that knows who you are and what amazing things you do.

There are ways I can teach you to get more clients and increase your income, and still feel ethical about how you do it. There is no avoiding it – you need to market your business to make sure it survives, but you don't have to feel rubbish about doing it.

By putting all the key principles together, you will be ready to **take effective action**. Please don't confuse being busy with effective action as they are two very different things. You can be as busy as you like, but if you are not being productive in the right areas, it is useless. Instead, take specific and effective action, which in turn will increase your productivity.

Structure will make your business function, so being clear on how you will work and when is essential. Without structure, you just create a scattergun approach to your marketing, which is never effective at getting you the results you desire. Timed tasks with no distractions, tracking of results, interim checks and adjusting as necessary are key.

My five simple principles will help you commit to your business and anything else you want to achieve in life. They will bring about big results, bring in more clients and increase your income.

I am known for my straight-talking, kick-butt and action-taking mentality. I am also a natural nurturer who loves to help. This may seem a strange combination, but it works well for me. I am fair minded, but I can spot excuses a mile off and I hate them. I am passionate and compassionate, but I do not believe in sugar coating the truth. Why? Because long term, if I tell you a sugar-coated fairy story, it just won't serve you. You will struggle to reach your goals. So I speak from my heart, 'kindly blunt' is a description that I feel is fair. Yes, it may feel uncomfortable at times, but all change feels that way, and I need you to make changes.

Ready? Then it's time to follow me through each principle, building your ability to commit to the success you want.

1
My Story

Before we start looking at the five principles in detail, I would like to tell you my story as a source of motivation and encouragement. Here goes.

Home

I grew up in a loving family that sheltered me from the realities of life. My parents were two hard-working people who never spoke of money worries, or any other difficulties. I had a fabulous childhood, and I just assumed everyone had had the same type of upbringing, and that life for me as a grownup would unfold in the same way.

My older sister was the slimmer, prettier and more intelligent one. She exuded confidence and personality, which I felt I didn't have. I looked up to her, as I still do, even though I am slightly taller! All in all, life was great at home and I am fortunate to still have strong links with my family.

School

At first, I enjoyed school, where there was a lot of emphasis on sport. This subject has been my true love from as early as I can remember. I was just five years old when I received all the swimming ribbons that were available at the school. Competitive even at that young age, I was a confident, chatty little girl and I adored my sports teacher. She formed a winning netball team that I excelled in and I still thank her for my love of all sports.

I learned to read early, but spelling and grammar were a lottery for me. Watching my son struggle in the same way, I suspect that I have some dyslexic traits, but that wasn't understood or tested for in my schooldays. I just ended up with a lot of red 'See Me's from the teachers in my workbooks.

Secondary school became more of a struggle for me. I was OK at most things, but it felt like I was always below average in academic subjects. Anything where I had to learn facts was hard for me; I did better when

I had to understand concepts. To learn, I had to be interested in and understand a subject. Rote learning was never going to be my thing, and it still isn't.

In secondary school, we were banded according to our perceived academic ability. I was put in the white band; the blue band was the bottom and the red band the top. I am not sure of the ratio for the split, but the white band was the largest band with the greatest variety of abilities within it. I felt lost in that band, not bright enough to deserve extra tuition and not struggling enough to warrant extra support. Being in the white band had a terrible effect on my confidence and I truly believed I had let my family down because I wasn't clever enough. The only subject I excelled and could show my fierce competitive nature in was PE.

My first 'I can, I will, watch me!' moment

There was one academic subject I liked: biology. I had an awesome teacher who believed in me and managed to get me moved up to the higher-ability class. Unfortunately, I was greeted in my first lesson there by the new teacher telling me I would never catch up with the work or pass the exam. On this occasion, though, instead of crushing my confidence, her comments made me mad. So mad that I decided I would rather die than fail. This was the first sign that I was a fighter and, when the right buttons were pushed, I could commit to achieving anything. I passed my biology exam and will always thank that unsupportive teacher for giving me the motivation to prove her wrong.

By this time, I was fifteen and it was time to think about a career. My school put on a careers evening – I don't remember there being much choice, but I really liked the idea of being a physiotherapist. Sadly, the teacher at the physiotherapy table, one of my subject teachers, was quick to tell me I would never make the grades. No discussion or advice on what I could do to achieve my dream; just a verbal slap and I was sent on my way.

After doing my exams, I decided that working all day at a desk was not for me. In my later teenage years, I was heavily into horses, so I decided to go off to agricultural college and train as a farm secretary. My work involved doing secretarial and book-keeping, naturally, along with driving a tractor, milking a cow and helping a sheep give birth.

At twenty-two years of age, I married a farmer, had my daughter at twenty-four, and three years later my son arrived. I thought I had the life I wanted. At that time, I was playing National League volleyball and I had worked my way up from the second team to the first team, playing for Ashcombe. This is where I discovered what strength I had and how being a team player was one of the most important skills I could learn. I was driven and committed to my training and my team. On the sports field, I was a completely different person. Little did I know then how useful being a competitive team player would be in the future.

The day it all changed

I can remember the day that I made the choice to change my life journey. It was a huge event for me, and a painful one.

I was playing at the Guernsey Open volleyball tournament. Each final was filmed for Guernsey TV, the coverage showing us running on to the court accompanied by pumping music and even a smoke machine. It wasn't glamorous.

As each player ran on court, we were introduced. I heard the expected 'Helen Bullen, number twelve, middle hitter', then came the words that haunted me and made me want more: 'Farmer's wife'. I can remember being horrified that I was categorised under my husband's job. I was surrounded by teammates with careers and qualifications, and suddenly I wanted more. I knew I could be more.

After the final, before we flew home, I had a long conversation with my coach. I have a lot to thank her for. She ignited my belief that I – the girl with limiting beliefs in her academic ability – could be more if I wanted it enough. In our chat, she encouraged me to think about training as a sports teacher, and I set off home determined to make some serious changes. I wasn't sure exactly how, but I was going to change my life path.

As it happened, I didn't go the route of teaching at that time. Instead, I studied sports massage and got hooked on manual therapy. One of my tutors was an osteopath, and from her I was inspired to learn more about osteopathy. When she sorted out an injury to my foot, I knew that osteopathy was the career for me.

Some serious home study covered the course work for an A level in human biology. I needed the qualification, so I committed to getting it. I got an interview to study at the college of my choice, and to my absolute surprise received an unconditional offer, despite my lack of the formal entry qualifications.

Four years on, I graduated as an osteopath. I had found a subject that I understood and was passionate about, which was when I discovered that I could learn when I was interested in a subject. I lived and breathed anatomy/physiology and pathology and I excelled in the clinic. Finally, I had found my niche. I wasn't average; I was good, and the exam results and patient feedback proved it.

After graduating, I was asked by the then principal to go back to teach at the college. I was fortunate enough that the college financed my teacher training, and three years later I was a fully qualified tutor too.

From being told at the age of fifteen I was not clever enough to be a physiotherapist, I became a fully qualified osteopath and a trained teacher. I enjoyed roles as vice principal and an international external examiner for three overseas osteopathic courses, along with a place on the governing body's investigating committee. During this time, I also opened an award-winning multi-healthcare clinic single-handedly.

Rock bottom

During the early days of running my first clinic, I was struggling. I had left my husband, I had two children and no child maintenance. I had a bucket of water instead of a fridge and an old microwave a friend had given me to cook with. It was so hard to get clients and make enough money to cover my rent and bills, let alone all the things the kids needed. I was desperate and alone.

I was using the 'sit, wait and hope' marketing technique, which is not a real technique at all. I will talk more about the sit, wait and hope method later in the book – particularly about how to avoid it.

I am, if nothing else, a fighter. I have always had the ability to feel like shit one minute and be planning a solution the next. Knowing I needed more cash, I decided to learn about marketing. I had to work it out fast or I would go under.

To help my cash flow, I took on an evening job a few nights a week as a rehab assistant and made time to learn how to market my business, get more clients and make a profit. After I'd worked hard to become a qualified teacher, I taught a few hours a week too, adding to my cash flow and making it possible to pay the essential bills as well as supporting my two children. I was starting to make ends meet, and gradually I discovered how to market my business effectively.

I worked my way up from rock bottom. In the early days, it really was just me, the kids and the bills. If I can do it, you can too. Anything is possible if you want it enough and you are prepared to work for it. I found out that I was better than average; I was strong. I had huge amounts of fight and common sense. Needing to make money, I had the greatest motivator: two children who needed me to make my life a success. I never gave up. Yes, I had ups and downs, but I fought hard and won.

Around 2009, I got an unexpected leg up. Someone wanted to invest in me. My hard work and tenacity had been noticed and another person believed in me.

I opened my multi-disciplinary practice – Fine Fettle Multi-healthcare. As I had a silent investor, I had full control of the business. It was around this time that I realised I had to do much more marketing for this bigger clinic. I now had others who relied on me pulling in clients and, with a large rent to pay, I needed to learn how to get a good income coming in.

I invested £1,000s in business coaches. Some were good, some not so good, and some were awesome, but I learned from all of them. The good and the awesome taught me things I put into action, and the not so good I put down as a learning curve and vowed never to coach like them. Having a natural flair for getting things done, I then started to develop my own methods. The good news was, once I started, I got the bug for business. I found it easy to learn about and I was good at it.

My favourite quote is from Arthur Ashe: 'Success is a journey, not a destination'. Your business is not a route that you travel and get to the end; instead, it is a constant process. You learn, you progress, you fall, you regroup, you become stronger. And most importantly, every step along the way is progress.

All it took for my change of circumstances was for someone to believe in me enough to see my strengths and support my weaknesses; to be my biggest cheerleader. I hope I can be that cheerleader for you, so keep reading. You can achieve anything you want to achieve, and I am here to show you how.

2
Care Of Self

L ook at the people who have achieved great things and the majority of them will have a story of self-care threaded throughout their journey. Waking early, exercise, eating well, positivity and huge amounts of self-belief – all elements that increase your chances of achieving the success you want.

The first of my five principles, 'care of self', is made up of a number of factors, and all are as important as each other. Just like a jigsaw puzzle, you need all the pieces to make the picture.

I was trained in key osteopathic principles that were founded in the late 1800s by Andrew Taylor Still, an American physician. Still was ahead of his time in realising that the human body is a unit that is an equal combination of body, mind and spirit. He believed that structure and function were linked and that treatment needed to be aimed at the whole body/mind complex and not just the musculo-skeletal system.

This is the reason I fell in love with osteopathy. The mind is underestimated in its ability to affect how the body works, and vice versa. If you neglect your body, it will have an effect on how you think and react. If you ignore the need to move regularly and fuel your body well, then you are missing a key element of your business and, let's face it, your life.

Why I made care of self a priority

I worked hard in my businesses, pushing forward constantly and hustling to make things work. This was effective to a point, but before long I realised that I was going to burn out if I didn't take care of myself in the process. I was constantly complaining of headaches and tired all the time, struggling to do things that I needed to do. Everything felt like an uphill climb. I put this down to the stress of work, but in reality, it was the lack of care I was taking of my own body. Happy to advise my patients, I had forgotten to take that advice myself. Sounds mad now, but at the time I thought I was too busy to eat well and exercise regularly. Have you found yourself thinking the same?

It can be so easy as a business owner to purely focus on getting new clients, making the next sale, filling funnels, Google ranking, etc, but as I found out, none of that gets you the results you could get if you looked after number one too. Omit this part and you are likely to find yourself on the road to overwhelm and lack of motivation.

I have been successful over the years, but I really started to get big traction on my success when I regarded my health and fitness as the number-one priority. My health had to come first, and I can honestly say as soon as I made sure it did, things just became so much easier. I committed to an early morning routine to enhance my health and wellbeing. I exercised daily and fuelled my body with good wholefood, drastically reducing my intake of sugar.

Feeling well from the inside will have a huge impact on your own self-worth, as well as the obvious health benefits. Care of self is important for you and your business, rather than something you choose to do if you get time. Change your thoughts about exercise and eating well, as wellbeing is the foundation of your business success.

Exercise

Exercise is essential for your body's health. Even the simplest of ten-minute walks will lift your mood, productivity and cognitive function. Exercise has been proven to reduce stress and anxiety, increasing your creativity and problem-solving ability. You will find it also increases your energy and boosts your confidence. Make exercise non-negotiable and see it as an integral part of success for you and your business.

CHALLENGE – THE TEN-MINUTE RULE

I use this technique on the days when I don't want to get up and move. Whatever I feel like, whatever the weather, whatever my day has been like, I have a rule that I must do a minimum of ten minutes of exercise.

Get your walking shoes on and get out the door. Put on a coat and wellies if it is raining, put on a sunhat if it is hot, but no excuses. Then walk or run for ten minutes. Once you have completed the ten minutes, you have the option to stop.

Whenever I have used this technique, I have never once turned around and come back after ten minutes. Once those endorphins kick in, I want to carry on.

What are you waiting for? Get out the door now. You will be so glad you did.

Mindset

There are so many advantages to creating a positive outlook on life. The first and most obvious is that it makes you feel good. Walking around with a positive outlook affects your physiology, releasing happy hormones like dopamine and serotonin. Smiling is enough to start the process. You may not feel like smiling, but do it. Do it now, and you will have tricked your brain into releasing a happy hormone.

Test this out by spending the rest of the day smiling at everyone you meet. Now you will have a double effect: you will increase your happiness and touch another person's world too. It's rare that someone will do anything but smile back at you. Your first lesson in positivity, and already you have improved your own and other people's wellbeing.

Be thankful for what you have

A great way to keep your focus on positivity is to show gratitude. What do you have that you are grateful for? Your health? Your family? That you have a roof over your head? That you have food and you are not afraid for your life?

Sometimes to focus on being grateful, it is important to go back to the basics. The reality is that you are probably living a great life compared to so many people. Does it matter that you don't have the car you dream of yet? Does it matter that you can't afford a trip to the Maldives? No. What matters is you have the basics that you need to survive. Be grateful – it is easy to forget how much you already have.

Appreciating what you have on a daily basis encourages your brain to focus on the positive. Being grateful takes seconds and, with practice, becomes a natural thing to do. Make it a habit and you will start to look at things in a positive light rather than negative. Negativity is never going to make you happy, get you more clients or earn you more income. It's a waste of your time.

Personally, I like to go through the things I am grateful for as soon as I wake in the mornings and last thing at night. A boost of positivity at the start and end of the day is a great way to increase my ability to deal with stress and put things into perspective.

Looking at life from the perspective of gratitude will increase your energy, your ability to make clear decisions and your problem-solving ability – all skills you need for your business. And as a bonus, these skills will filter into the whole of your life. Living your life in a pity party is a waste of your time and energy. Negative thoughts narrow your focus and stop you from growing both personally and in business. They don't serve you and are likely to repel those around you. On the other hand, positivity pulls like-minded people towards you. These people encourage you, support you and love you for your attitude.

In short, positivity helps you focus clearly on your business without negativity limiting your every decision.

CHALLENGE – THE FIVE-MINUTE GRATITUDE HABIT

Take five minutes every morning and evening to develop your gratitude habit. You can think, write, say things out loud that you are grateful for. These can be people, possessions, places, emotions – anything you choose. Notice how showing gratitude for them changes your mood, especially when you realise how much you have to be grateful for and how good it is to put things into perspective.

Try it now. Think of five things that you are grateful for and why. Start this process by thinking/saying/writing 'Today I am grateful for...' five times and enjoy filling in the rest.

Monitor negative self-talk

What would you do if a close friend came up to you and said you were stupid? I am sure you would be hurt and upset, and maybe question your friendship. Why, then, do you allow yourself to say those types of things to yourself?

We likely all have heard the voice, the inner critic, that for some reason has decided it is OK to speak to us in the most vile and horrible fashion. It questions our ability, tells us things will never work. It may even say we are useless. That voice is ours, but we still allow it to say the meanest things. We let it freely undermine how we feel and tell us things that we would not forgive anyone else for saying.

It can be too easy to continually tell ourselves nasty things, like 'I am so stupid' or 'I am fat' or 'I am ugly'. These are really mean things to say, so why do we talk to ourselves in this way?

It is important to remember that there is only one person who will be with you 100% of the time from the day you are born to the day you die. That person, of course, is you. There is no getting away from yourself, and if you are constantly being nasty to yourself, it's not a nice way to live. It is time to stop being nasty. Stop using negative and derogatory talk aimed at yourself. Instead, show yourself love and care.

Start today by listening to your thoughts directed at yourself. Monitor the negative and nasty comments, and remind yourself that you must be kind. After all, I'm sure you are kind to your friends and family and clients, so why is it OK to be nasty to yourself? It is certainly not helping your business.

Feed your brain with positivity

A great way to counter negative self-talk is to train your brain to hear positivity daily. First, you need to recognise when you are being mean to yourself and change how you speak to yourself. The next thing you do is to feed your brain with positivity.

Affirmations are statements confirming something is true. Positive affirmations are good at instantly improving your mood, and your mind will absorb your kind words. I think of affirmations as ways to say 'Well done!' to my mind, to congratulate it for being so awesome and to cheer it on to greater and better things. I promise it feels much better saying nice things to yourself than nasty. Give it a go and see how you find it.

CHALLENGE – AFFIRMATIONS

Here are some examples of simple positive affirmations. You can choose to use these or create your own. I like to keep affirmations short so I can remember them easily and repeat them throughout the day, but you could make yours longer and more specific:

- I am brilliant
- I achieve everything I want to achieve
- I commit to tasks I need to get done
- I am in control of my feelings, both positive and negative
- I am in control of my own happiness

I recommend that you repeat your affirmations daily. When you get up, say them either to yourself or out loud, and give yourself a little positive boost throughout the day by repeating them. Write them on a sticky note and display them proudly on the wall as a reminder. You can choose a new one every day or stick to ones you know work for you. Mix it up, smile and enjoy the feeling of positivity.

Watch out as in the beginning, your mind may try to tell you that your affirmations aren't true. Shut that negative story off straight away. You can choose to listen to either the negative inner critic or the positive pom-pom waving cheerleader. I know what goes on in my head, and it involves plenty of whoop-whoops, somersaults and, of course, glittery pom-poms.

Journaling

I like to journal, and I encourage those I work with to commit to this incredible discipline too. Getting into daily journaling can be a huge asset for your own self-care as it releases emotions and gives you mental clarity. It can be done in just a few minutes or over a longer period of time, there are no set rules. For me, a ten-minute journal time is perfect. You can use it to solve problems, encourage positivity and set yourself up for the day.

Take a blank page in a notebook and your favourite pen. You can use a document on your digital device, but I recommend a beautiful notebook with clean pages and eye-catching cover. Grab the pen that writes the most smoothly and feels good in your hand. Find a place to write that makes you feel comfortable. Clear your emotions, get clarity, and let your journal be your therapist and confidant.

You can free write in your journal, just getting things out of your head on to the page. Don't wallow in negativity; instead, make your journal a place for positivity, gratitude, ideas and creativity. A place for inspiration and motivation to help you feel ready to take on your day.

Another way to journal, if you find free writing difficult, is to have prompts. Here are some ideas to get things going that I like, but you are free to create your own:

- Dear past me...

- Dear future me...

- Today I will be grateful for...

- What change could I make to my business that excites me?

Journaling will really help to transform your mindset. What have you got to lose except a ton of negativity?

Making time for you

Working hard all the time is a trap many business owners fall into. Lack of planning and poor time management lead to the misconception that working as hard as you can must be the way to get you the success you dream of. Life is for living. Yes, your business is part of that living, but it should never take over.

When I started out working for myself, I thought I needed to work all the time. No breaks, no holidays, and I had to do it all. This worked to a point, but over time, it led to me feeling exhausted, mentally drained and out of love with my business.

I decided that I was going to live my life the way I wanted to. No more struggle, anxiety and limiting myself to a life of hard work. Instead, I was going to achieve what I wanted in my business, and that included having more time off to do all the things I wanted to do with my life.

Working all the time will be detrimental to your business rather than beneficial, so please take time to rethink how you work. Being constantly on call to customers with little structured time off is a sure way to stress and overwhelm. Instead, plan your day so that you can finish work earlier and spend more time with your loved ones. Don't *ever* sacrifice relationships for work.

Set structured hours for seeing clients. The biggest mistake you can make with your day is to be on call all the time, just in case someone needs to see you. You then spend the whole day waiting instead of dividing it into specific work times. I would advise that you leave a few hours available in your diary each week for out-of-hours appointments (eg at the weekend or in the evening), but on the whole, don't be scared to set your hours. You won't lose clients or money – clients don't need a vast amount of choice on appointment times, so give yourself more free time. If your business gets so busy that you need to expand into more hours, you can always consider getting someone in to help.

Don't get caught up in the thinking that to be good, you have to show everyone around that you work a lot of hours. You control your business, not the other way around, but until you acknowledge this, you are likely to stay stuck in an overworked, stressed and overwhelmed state. Busy does not equate to success; instead, success equates to having a business that you are in control of and love.

Taking time off is essential to reset your energy levels. It will increase your productivity and success in all areas of your life. Don't ignore the signs that you need to take some downtime, and remember your business will benefit too. Do things that make you smile, laugh, sing or even dance (I am going to positively encourage you to dance). Commit to your own happiness and wellbeing, and schedule regular time to do the things you want to do. Whatever floats your boat – you can take that literally or figuratively.

CHALLENGE – JUST STOP

When you feel in control of your time, you will feel great, so stop reading. Sit and do nothing for ten minutes. This is time just for you.

This is a great habit to get into and one that I would recommend you do every day. You will be amazed at the recharging effect ten minutes can have. Go do it!

3
Know Your Why

It can be easy to trudge along through life, accepting what you have as your 'lot'; easy to forget dreams and aspirations that you used to have; easy to put up with where you are and push back thoughts of doing things differently. It can be even easier to think that you can't have the success you crave and that good fortune only happens to others.

I am going to urge you, right now, to think about what you want. I mean *really* want. What dreams did you once have that you have given up on? Do you look at others and think you can't have what they have? Perhaps you don't think you are worthy of your dreams, or you believe that you are not good enough to reach them?

You have to know the reason why you run your business. What do you intend for that business? How will you commit to pushing forward with all your dreams and ideas? Problems arise when you lose track of what you really want. Then what you get instead of your dream business is a watered-down version, full of compromise and, in many cases, regret.

My second principle, knowing the 'why' of your business, needs to underlie everything you do. You must want your why strongly enough. Are you hoping success will happen or are you actively figuring out how to make it happen? The difference between figuring it out and relying on hope is a successful business that you love or one that disappoints. Hoping has never worked for anyone, but figuring it out has a high success rate. And to figure it out, you need to know the why behind it all.

When did you last sit down and plan your business journey according to what you want? It could be that over time, your business has turned into something you now don't recognise. You may have got so caught up working in your business that you've never stepped back and checked why you are running it that way.

Having your dream business is up to you. You can achieve it, but your why needs to be solid and strong. You need to assume full responsibility for the journey your business goes on and take measures to ensure you are always moving towards your dream, not drifting towards a compromise.

Commitment is key to your success. It is what I have used to get everything I have ever wanted, always planning, reacting to change and setbacks in a positive way, and living a life that I love.

Climb into the driving seat of your business and move it forward. Don't expect it to stay the same; instead, regularly check and adjust it where you need to. Not every day of your business life will be easy. There will be curveballs thrown at you regularly, but when you have a why that is strong, it's easy to throw those balls straight back.

Reignite your passion

Do you remember the first days of building your business? The excitement and the belief that it was going to be totally awesome? You probably spent hours planning, sorting, creating and generally living and breathing your new business; you could think of nothing else. You were proud to tell everyone about it and you knew why you had started it. You had vision, you had enthusiasm and you had passion.

Now the reality. How do you feel today about your business? Are you still in that honeymoon phase or are you thinking of getting a divorce?

I know the feeling of falling out of love with a business. The things that used to excite you no longer sing. Your business seems to be nothing but hard work and time consuming. You wonder how you ever had the confidence to start it and why it feels like you are constantly chasing different ways to make money rather than sticking to your original ideas. You have lost confidence in your ability and belief that you can have a successful therapy business.

Your business is a bit like a relationship. The initial euphoria of being with a new person wears off, just like the enthusiasm for a new business can. The reality is not what you hoped for, so you try to change things until you no longer recognise the business you first planned. You have made your business into some muddled model, you have forgotten the initial joy, you lack clients, and it is sapping all your time, self-confidence and money.

If that was a relationship you would have two choices – get a divorce or get some counselling. I am hoping that you are not ready to jack it all in and divorce your business, but just need to reignite the passion.

CHALLENGE – WHAT DO YOU REALLY WANT?

Imagine what your ideal business would look like. Imagine how you would feel. Imagine how many days a week you would work. Imagine where you would work.

Don't let your mind jump in and tell you it won't be possible or that it can't work; just let your creative mind run free. It's time to reignite that passion.

Would you be working from home three days a week? Would you be seeing twenty clients per week, or are you ambitious and wanting to own a chain of clinics? Are you happy with four weeks off a year, or do you want more? What do you dream of?

When you have answered those questions, think about how you would fund your dream business. How long would it take you to achieve it and what steps do you need to take to get you there? What parts are realistic and what parts need to stay as just ideas for now?

It can be all too easy to drift along, wishing you had your ideal business but never taking decisive action. If you want your dream business, you need to know exactly what those dreams are. You can reach your goals, but you have to know where you are heading and then plan how you will get there.

Take some time today to sit down and remember all the things you wanted from your business when you set it up. Get yourself some sticky notes or a notebook and go through all those ideas, plotting them out. Brain dumping is the best way I know to get ideas from dream to reality, so that is exactly what we will be covering in the next section.

Brain dump

This is not a new technique, but it is one you can go back to time and time again to help you sort out ideas and actions. It can be used throughout the life of your business, not just for the initial planning; for big projects as well as really small ones. Brain dumping will produce awesome results and save you time too.

A brain dump is quite self-explanatory – you dump everything that is going round in your brain on to paper, and then arrange it into a sensible order. I love to brain dump for weekly planning to break large tasks into a clear to-do list. It helps when I have decisions to make, when I can't think straight, when I feel overwhelmed and when a task just seems too big.

To brain dump, you first need to get ideas and thoughts out of your overcrowded brain. The best way to do this is to buy some sticky notes (get the good ones that actually stick). They can be small, large, colourful or plain, but get a stack of them.

Pick the subject you are going to brain dump. It could be a large subject like your whole business, your life or your fitness, or it could be something smaller like a marketing campaign, your accounts or ways to get new clients through your door. The most important part of a brain dump, and probably the hardest thing to do when you start, is not to hold back. Don't limit your freedom with thoughts that tell you something's impossible, it's too expensive or that it's going to be too hard. Just get every last idea out of your head. This is *your* brain dump – who cares if one of your ideas is to be a unicorn trainer? You will have time once you have dumped to filter and check each idea; making decisions at this point will just stop your creative flow. Get all those ideas out; you will be amazed how good it feels.

I love seeing what I let escape from my head. Who knew I wanted to run business retreats in Thailand until I brain dumped on all the things I thought I was capable of? Who knew that I had a passion for singing until I brain dumped that I wanted to start singing lessons?

Here is a word of warning for your brain dump. If you have a break at any point, take a photo of your sticky notes. Notes can get blown away, knocked off a surface or cleared up by a helpful family member – yes, that has happened to me! Just like you would save a document on your computer, do the same here.

Sit down today and get all those ideas and dreams out of your head on to paper. Enjoy the feeling of dreaming about what you truly want. Allow yourself to be free and to put down *everything*.

I actually prefer to stand and use a large blank wall area to do my brain dump, but you may find you like to dump while sitting at a desk. Whatever you do, make sure it feels good to you and allows you to be creative and free with your ideas.

Next you need to put those notes with your brilliant ideas into order, which is why I recommend using sticky notes – they're easy to rearrange. The order depends on the outcome you are looking for. If you are looking to make more money, then you need to prioritise any ideas that will help increase your income short term. If you have things that are time sensitive, you will need to order them into time priority. Each brain dump will have a different purpose, so order it according to the outcome you want, but remember to put the notes that will make you happy and fulfilled at the top, and list other things below.

CHALLENGE – TIME TO BRAIN DUMP

- Pick a subject.
- Scribble every single idea you have on that subject on to sticky notes. Let your mind run wild; don't stop to think if an idea is a good or a bad one. Just write each thought on a separate sticky note.
- Stick all those sticky notes over a clear surface. Now is the time to put them in some sort of order. Because you have used sticky notes, you can freely move them around, tear some up, add some and generally sort your brain dump. It's amazing how quickly things become clear.
- You may find that you have to pick a few of your sticky notes and go again on the brain dump. Breaking things down into bite-size chunks is a much better way to get things sorted.

Don't dismiss brain dumping before you try it. I promise you it will save you so much time and eliminate procrastination, as this story from my own experience shows.

When I was setting out my key principles, I was away with my coach in Thailand. I was tired and had run out of my favourite 90% chocolate. For me, that equates to seriously tough times.

The task given to me by my coach seemed too overwhelming. I put the notebook down and went out to the lounger on the balcony and told myself I could sleep if I wanted to. Five minutes later, my brain was on super charge. When I get like that it is as if I have voices in my head. I knew what to do: I needed to set the scene for me to be creative. Sticky notes and my favourite marker pens came out of my bag (never travel without the essentials, I say). I turned my phone on to a good playlist, looked around the room for a suitable wall, and boom! I was back in the creative game.

Ninety minutes later and after a lot of brain dumping, my core model 'Commit to Achieve' had been born. It made me laugh as every step that I had used to get the job done was exactly what I was going to teach in my model. I had taken care of myself, I knew why I had to do it, I had addressed any limiting beliefs and mapped it out logically and fully. I understood what needed doing and I had taken effective action.

Just as I was stepping back to admire my work, in walked my coach. This guy was incredible at knowing when to search me out and check in on me. Well, I was ready. The plan was awesome, and I had totally proved why my skills lie in committing to getting a job done. I am thankful to say he was impressed too.

Brain dumping allowed me to focus my thoughts. Don't ever underestimate the power of a brain dump, the freedom to create and the fast results you will get. Brain dumping can be used for any problem solving or creative exercise, for a large area or a small one. I use it all the time, from planning my social media to creating a webinar for my coaching clients. Get yourself some sticky notes today and see what happens when you let your mind run free.

A clinic ethos

Even before I set up my clinic, I'd decided I wanted it to operate in a certain way and I needed my colleagues to work with me to create a collegiate and professional atmosphere. Most importantly, I wanted a clinic where we could all enjoy working to provide the best care possible for all of our clients. So I set about writing my own unique clinic ethos.

It's important to set out the why for your business clearly for yourself and others. Setting the scene early is easier than trying to bring it in later on. I call it an ethos, but you could call it a plan or guide. You can put anything in your ethos, but it needs to be applicable to staff, associates and clients. You need everyone buying into your why.

My wish was to set up a multi-disciplinary practice to integrate a wide variety of complementary treatments. My vision was to have a practice where all the therapists worked together for the benefit of the patient. I didn't want a clinic with four rooms, therapists all working separately. Instead I wanted us to work together to provide the best care we could for our patients. We all had to understand what each therapist did and which therapies complemented each other best.

I believe that you should treat patients in a way that you would want to be treated yourself, at all times. I decided I didn't want a clinic with rushed appointments; I would rather have quality over quantity. I truly believe that if we integrate and give our best care to all patients, the business income will add up itself without shortened appointments and half-hearted care.

All patients have the right to know what to expect from treatment and be fully aware that they can ask questions at any time or withdraw their consent. All patients have the right to expect a full consultation, expert examination, a well-assessed diagnosis and professional treatment. In my clinic, we are qualified frontline practitioners and must have in-depth knowledge of pathology with excellent case-history-taking skills to ensure patient safety. We must also have the ability to recognise any conditions outside of our area of expertise and refer patients immediately to another practitioner or GP as appropriate.

In my experience, the best way of advertising is good patient referral. This should drive us all to treat every person as an individual and give them our best professional attention at all times.

CHALLENGE – CREATE YOUR OWN ETHOS

An ethos is useful whether you work as a sole practitioner or with multiple therapists. It is essential to be clear with your vision for the business – your why – and to share it with others so that they are fully informed.

It's time to sit down and create your own clinic ethos. I encourage you to make sure it reflects your own aspirations, but you can use mine as a guide.

Love Monday, embrace Wednesday, and get excited on Sunday

Whatever business you create, it is really important that you enjoy it. It must be your passion rather than a chore.

So many people in their working life live for Friday and dread Sunday evening as they get ready to restart a week of work. You are going to work for many years of your life, so you need to love what you do. My mantra is this: love Monday, embrace Wednesday, and get excited on Sunday.

Monday is always exciting. It is a new start to the week and a time to look at ideas and focus on new things. I love a Monday. Wednesday is often called 'hump day', implying you've got over the hump and are on the downward path to the weekend. If you feel like this every week, you need to seriously take a look at your business. Why spend your life wishing the days away every week to get to Friday, and then dreading the arrival of Monday? Wednesday to me is just like having another Monday: a fresh start if I need it, or time to continue pushing forward with my business, but not a day that simply gets me closer to the weekend.

Over the years of building my coaching business, I felt it was important to embrace Wednesday as a positive day. I tried to come up with some clever alliterations like Wishful Wednesday or Wonderful Wednesday, but none felt quite right until a friend called it Woohoo Wednesday. The name stuck, and for me it will always be Woohoo Wednesday. Why not make your Wednesday a woohoo type of day?

Sunday is another day you need to watch out for. If you are not totally in love with your business, you will find that by Sunday evening, you will be dreading the arrival of Monday morning. Many people lose half of their Sunday to feeling terrible. If you have a business you love, Sunday becomes a day to spend with family or doing the things you enjoy, and at the end of the day, you will actually be excited by the prospect of another week.

How does Sunday feel to you? If you are dreading the start of a new week, it really is time to make some changes. Life is not about rushing from Monday to Friday every week, wishing the weekend would hurry up and arrive. Most people spend at least a third of their life working, so it is important to create a business you love working in. If you love your work, it won't feel like work, and that really is the way to live.

Take a look at your working week. Do you need to make changes to create a business that you really love?

Reverse engineering your goals

You want success, you have spent time working out what you want your business to be like, but that is not enough to make it happen. You need to plan your journey. Perhaps you want to earn £60,000 per year or work three days a week. Perhaps you want to earn enough to pay your rent and go on two holidays a year. This is *your* why, so make is specific to you.

Reverse engineering is a great method for achieving your goals once you have set them. Instead of starting from where you are now, look from where you want to be and work back from there, plotting targets as you go.

Work out the timescale you are reverse engineering, for example three years, eighteen months or ninety days. Set your goal and work back through the journey – all the things you will need to do, targets to hit, etc. You could use a spreadsheet, diary or a large calendar on your wall – whatever works for you.

If you are working on increasing your income, work out the income you need to have made to hit each target on the path to your goal. My advice is to work this out quarterly, monthly and weekly. How many clients do you need to see to get to those quarterly, monthly and weekly targets? Make an action plan and stick to it.

Reverse engineering a goal is a great method, but please don't forget that the most important part of reaching a goal is to be consistent on the journey. Take the action to get there. Don't start and then peter out after a few weeks. You may need to tweak your plans as you go, but don't stop. See Chapter 9 – 'Take Effective Action' to help you structure your efforts.

Goals are great as they make you commit to getting things done, but remember that although you may do your best, there will be times when you don't get to your goal as planned. Business is not a simple process, but it is an exciting one. Obstacles you were not expecting will get in your way and you may even change your direction, but remember that even if you don't quite reach your goal as expected, you have moved closer. Everything you have done towards your goal will have pushed your business further forward. You will have learned along the way and taken action. Step up, reset and go again, all the time keeping your focus on your all-important why.

4

Release Your Limiting Beliefs

It may be that your business is struggling right now and you wish you had more clients and more income. You may have tried everything you can think of, but still you can't make ends meet and your business feels more like a hobby than anything that would make you a decent living. But here is the truth: *you* are the problem with your business.

Before you get defensive, listen up. If you know the truth, you can make changes, right? I am never going to sugar coat things or tell you what you want to hear; instead, I want to make an impact on you and your business. I want you to get what you want.

I have worked with many therapists and small business owners over the years, and after a while I came to realise that just knowing the marketing you need to do for your business is not enough to persuade you to take action and get results. If it was as simple as just learning marketing methods, then you'd have the successful business you want right now, wouldn't you? Something far larger and far harder to master is getting in the way – limiting beliefs.

Nearly all the business owners I have worked with have had beliefs that stopped them building the business they want. Beliefs they are not good enough; fear of being an imposter; fear of what others will say; negative beliefs about money and what they can earn. Take some time to recognise your own limiting beliefs as they are not serving you or your business. They mean that you really are the problem in your business, but the good news is that this means you are in control. You can change your thoughts and preconceived ideas. You have the power to shape a business you love that gets you results you want. How exciting is that?

Imposter syndrome

Imposter syndrome is a limiting belief that can strike at any time in your life. It makes you feel like everyone else is better and has more experience than you. This inner voice – the constant struggle between going for the success you dream of and feeling like a fraud who knows nothing, despite your qualifications and experience – can rock your confidence and make you doubt everything you do. Imposter syndrome can easily make you stressed, anxious and overwhelmed, and can even destroy your belief that you can push your business forward. Fear of getting 'found out' can stop you in your tracks. And it's so common – we all likely suffer from imposter syndrome in one shape or form, but it definitely won't help anyone's business in any way.

The inner critic goes to town with imposter syndrome, telling you to ignore compliments about the great work you do, that people are just being polite. It assures you that everyone else is more qualified than you, more experienced. Imposter syndrome can creep into your head because of what people have said to you in the past. If you feel like it's arrogant or showing off to promote yourself, it is likely that someone told you that when you were younger. It doesn't mean they were right, but it shows how the feelings of being an imposter can creep up on you.

Imposter syndrome is a falsehood, and the truth is, it is made up by you. You repeat limiting beliefs to yourself so often that you start to see them as the truth. But you have created the thoughts that you're not good enough. You have imagined others are better than you or more experienced without any evidence. You try to guess what others think of you, and you think it must be negative, not positive, but mind reading doesn't work.

Stop believing your made-up story of what others think. It is a lie, and the sooner you recognise that, the sooner your imposter feelings will subside. The truth is you are awesome; you are worthy of success.

CHALLENGE – BE NICE TO YOURSELF

I can't cure you of imposter syndrome, but you can. Here is how to tackle it.

If you are struggling with imposter syndrome, write down all the good qualities you have, your positive attributes and qualifications. This list is only for your eyes, so don't let your inner voice get a look in and tell you to hold back. Just write it all down. Now read it through and visually take in how much you know.

It can be easy to be cursed by knowledge. You are so used to the immense amount that you know, you forget others do not share that same knowledge. You have trained, you have learned and you are more than good enough to do your job. Yes, you need to be professional and know your limitations and be safe, but you also need to remember that you are an expert in what you do. Only you can be you, and that is your biggest sales point.

Don't let that inner critic tell you anything other than the real truth. As the philosopher Bertrand Russell wrote:

'The whole problem with the world is that
fools and fanatics are always so certain
of themselves, and wiser people so full of
doubts.'

Limiting beliefs about money

I had limiting beliefs around money – beliefs that
were preventing me from reaching my full potential.
I didn't like money. In fact, I hated it! It had negative
connotations for me relating to hardship, lack and
struggle.

After I'd ended up as a single parent, money became
an issue. It became a thing I had to have to survive. It
became a noose around my neck that tightened whenever I needed anything. Money came into my account
and left faster than I wanted it to. It hung around me
like a bad smell, a toxic part of my world. I became
fearful of money, of both having it and not.

I watched a film called *I, Daniel Blake*. There is a scene
in this film where the lead female character is lying
in bed with her daughter. In this scene, her daughter
asks for a new pair of school shoes because she has
grown out of the old ones. Her mum's face tells it all –
she is on benefits, struggling to get by, and she has no
way of getting enough money together for new shoes.

I cried for a few hours after watching this film. Why? Because that was once me – the mum who was asked by her daughter for new dance shoes because her second-hand ones were too small. I was the mum who sobbed that night as I just didn't have the money to give my daughter what other children around her had. In fact, I am getting upset just typing this.

Many of you may have experienced similar issues with money that could be holding you back, too. You may feel guilt for charging for what you do, undervaluing the impact you have on people's lives. But remember, you are helping people, providing a much-needed service.

Ask yourself, 'Am I undercharging?' I suspect the answer may be yes. Undercharging stems from a money-related limiting belief. You find it difficult to take payment for what you do, despite offering a good service. But there is an easy way around this problem and, as always with limiting beliefs, it is all around mindset.

CHALLENGE – CHARGE WHAT YOU'RE WORTH

Instead of thinking you're taking money for what you do, think of the service that you provide. People have a choice whether to come to see you, so make sure you give them great treatment and overserve them with excellent customer care. Be up front and proud about your charges. You will then attract clients who value what you do, and expect to pay well for it.

If you are confident that you are providing a much-needed service, then charging what you are worth will not be a problem.

Fear of failure

How often has fear of failure held you back? Stopped you from even starting things you want to achieve? Fear of failure is a common limiting belief, but you can change the way you think about failure.

It is likely that failure has a negative connotation in your head. Fear of failure is often linked to previous experiences when you haven't achieved what you wanted, and all the associated negative emotions: disappointment, embarrassment, etc. The key is to know that when you fail, you also learn – fast.

To fail is inevitable, so teach yourself to think about failure as a learning experience. Even if it does seem negative at the time, it will teach you things you need to know to avoid similar situations. Even better, it will likely show you which direction you need to take.

At the end of my second year of training to be an osteopath, I went into clinic to start treating my own clients under the guidance of my tutors. On one particular day, I had gone through the usual process of taking a case history and doing examinations, and I was halfway through my treatment with my client when my tutor leapt up, shouted for me to stop, and then verbally ripped into me, in front of the client, about using the wrong arm hold. I felt bad, the client was in shock, and I can remember shaking as I started again using the correct procedure.

Needless to say my attempt was not the best, but the important point is that I learned from this error. The tutor handled it badly, but I still learned – so much so that even today, nearly twenty years on, I relive part of that moment when I line up a client for the same treatment. That experience of failure made me a far better and safer practitioner – and I learned *never* to treat a student like that tutor had treated me when I became a clinic tutor myself!

Everyone can fear failure, but we will all fail at points throughout our lives, and we all still have some failures to come. But if you have a mindset that always gets back up, dusts yourself off and goes again, getting stronger as you go, you will achieve what you want in life. You only have to look at the amount of successful entrepreneurs who failed big time before they found success, from Walt Disney who was told by his newspaper editor that he lacked imagination, to James Dyson making well over 5,000 failed prototypes of his famous vacuum cleaner model, to Stephen Spielberg being rejected – twice – by the University of Cinematic Arts, California, to Oprah Winfrey who was fired from her first TV job as an anchor in Baltimore.

Time to restructure your mindset and see failure as simply learning. Yes, some failure may seem painful, but if you believe you can move forward from anything, then you will come out the other side stronger and more ready to take on your goals. Failure is a problem for you only when it stops you taking action. But here is the crux of the matter: you have already failed if you don't try due to fear of failure. It may seem comfortable staying where you are and never pushing yourself forward, but success and failure are linked because both take action to happen.

CHALLENGE – WHAT IS THE BEST THAT CAN HAPPEN?

Change your mindset to focus on positive outcomes. What could you achieve if you pushed yourself forward? Of course, risk assess to make sure that you have the things you need in place, eg cash flow and time, but don't be overzealous with your risk assessing. Just be fair and logical.

Ask yourself, 'Am I not stepping out of my comfort zone because the risk of failure is extremely high, or is it because I am self-sabotaging, being a perfectionist or not caring enough?' Only you can answer those questions.

Change your perception of the word 'failure'. Perhaps you could call it something different, like learning. Learning is the key to your success, so embrace the times things don't go quite to plan and move on stronger and wiser.

How others can affect your limiting beliefs

Do you ever come across people who diss everything you do? You know the types: they sneer at every idea you have, deride the things you plan to do and actively seek to belittle your dreams. These types of people can be described as drains. They drain your enthusiasm, your ideas, and eat away at your self-esteem.

Motivational speaker Jim Rohn famously said, 'You are the average of the five people you spend the most time with.' Maybe it's time to ask yourself who you are hanging around with. Think hard and prepare for some changes if necessary.

CHALLENGE – SURROUND YOURSELF WITH RADIATORS

Look at the people around you. Are they supportive or negative?

Positive and supportive people can be likened to radiators. They inspire you, motivate you, encourage you and give constructive feedback to your ideas. They don't knock you down simply to make themselves feel better about where they are in life. Instead, they actively embrace your brilliance and go out of their way to support and cheerlead you on your way. You will automatically know who the radiators are as you enjoy being with them.

Attract more radiators into your world. Surround yourself with people who get you, who support you and like you.

I am not saying you have to fire all your friends, but choose wisely, and hang out for longer with those who radiate positive energy, inspire you and boost your confidence. Give little or no time to those who drain you. It can be liberating once you try it.

Banish excuses

I don't believe your excuses. I don't believe you. Yes, really! It is time to stop making excuses for why you don't have what you want.

I am talking about the constant reasons that many people give themselves for not taking action to get to their goals. You may have people around you who buy into your excuses and positively encourage you to make them, but I am not going to be one of those people. I am going to be the person who actively helps you get to your goals and dreams rather than reinforcing the excuses that are holding you back.

Excuses are easy to make and even easier to action, but life happens to us all. You may be going through a divorce; you may have loads of work to do; you may be a single parent; you may even have health problems. We all have issues we need to deal with, but please don't use them as excuses not to move towards where you want to be. Don't throw them in the way of success. You may have to change your route a little and work with and around some of the things that life throws at you, but never give up on your dreams.

Excuses are easy to spot when they are not your own. When people say they can't meet up with you or get into work early, you're likely to know instantly if their reason is valid or just an excuse. So why pretend your own excuses are any more believable? I would like to encourage you to see your excuses as just another challenge to overcome, and you *can* overcome it. You just need to prioritise what is really important and you will soon work out how.

Excuses can only hold you back and get in your way; they will never help you get to where you want to go. In truth, they are a waste of your time and energy. If you want to get fit, get out the door and start training. Start slowly, but start. If you want to lose weight, change how you eat. It is not a part-time solution and something that can be picked up and put down. Make changes and stick to them. I changed my eating and exercise habits, and I am proud to say that I have not only reached my fitness goals, I also stick to the plan for the majority of the time. I have changed my outlook and I am in it for the long term.

Listen to yourself when you make excuses like 'I will start next week' or 'I can't because I am just not in the right head space'. Those types of excuses may feel like valid reasons, but they are just limiting beliefs keeping you in the place you are now, and ultimately you will never reach your goal if you listen to them. Don't allow yourself to believe your excuses. Instead, work out a way to get started, and then *always* start straight away.

Achieving goals for the life of your business takes a long-term mindset. Switching your marketing on and off will not get you the outcomes you wish for. Waiting until 'it is a good time' will not get you the business you want. Tough talking, I know, but I want to get you out of any short-term mindset. Action in the short term is a waste of your time and effort; your business needs you to take action now and for the rest of its life. No excuse is ever going to help your business, so it's time to stop using them.

CHALLENGE – TACKLE YOUR OWN EXCUSES

Think about an excuse you have been using that is stopping you moving forward in your business. Dig deep into this excuse and ask yourself what the truth behind it is.

Take the excuse and break it down. What is it stopping you doing...? Eg you 'don't have time' to market your business on a regular basis.

For this excuse – lack of time – look at the time you have in your day and recognise that you have 24 hours to get things done. What exactly is behind this excuse? Do you spend too much time on Netflix and scrolling on social media or do you waste time between clients and over your lunch hour? Perhaps you lack knowledge and confidence about what you need to do so you are never motivated or try to avoid making proper time.

Work through any excuse in the same way and look for the underlying cause. It may be a limiting belief, like fear of failure or imposter syndrome. It may be lack of knowledge or procrastination.

Once you uncover the real reason you can then work on that to avoid putting excuses in your way. Go back through the Commit to Achieve principles to help you.

The drama behind limiting beliefs

I love this quote by Charles R Swindoll:

'Life is 10% what happens to you and 90% how you react to it.'

It is so true, so bear this in mind at all times, especially if you feel things are unfair or unjust. Focusing on the 90% will get you great results.

I know I can be guilty of a bit of drama, but it wasn't until I worked with one of my coaches that I realised how much of a drama queen I could be when it came to my business. Things will inevitably happen in your business that throw you off-kilter – things that can frustrate you, increase your stress levels and make you wonder why you do what you do. 'Woe is me' thoughts and feelings of negativity abound when something doesn't work or go as you planned – yes, I suffer from it too, but for a long time I didn't realise that I was making those feelings worse. Drama is literally drama – you are acting out a situation, but what if you could control it?

My coach stepped in one day when I was mithering over a difficult work situation. I was not impressed; I wanted sympathy to show me he agreed how difficult it was for me. Instead, he just told me straight to cut the drama. No other advice; no contacting me to reassure me I could get through things.

Once I had got over my initial 'I hate you, why don't you understand what I am going through?' reaction, I realised he *had* given me advice. It was solely down to me to choose how I reacted to situations. I was in full control and had the power to remain calm and logical, or turn into a diva and throw a tantrum. This was one of those light-bulb moments for me that has served me well moving forward.

We all have to deal with difficult situations, but it can be done more efficiently if we take the emotion out of it. Things just seem easier then.

If you find that every day you are stressed, anxious and miserable, then you need to think your way out of it. You will have curveballs thrown at you, and some will feel like iron balls that hit you head on, but it is really important to know that only you can control how you react. I am not saying don't have a cry, a shout or a rant, but if you catch yourself creating even more drama, get yourself back in order quickly. Remind yourself that making a drama out of a crisis is not going to serve you well.

Personally, I allow myself five to ten minutes maximum of ranting (under my breath) and feeling sorry for myself. On occasions, I even allow myself a few tears, but then I stop. I shut off the emotion of the situation and work out how I can resolve the issue.

CHALLENGE – CUT THE DRAMA

Here are some tips for cutting the drama:

- Realise life is always going to be full of curveballs just waiting to fly at you. They will happen, and some may come one after another.

- You have control over your reactions, no one else. You have the ability to pick yourself up and take action. They may be small steps to begin with, but keep taking one step after another. I promise each one will be easier than the last.

You have no limits – unless you believe you have

Something as simple as baking a cake nearly sent my Facebook group into meltdown.

Running your business is all about taking action and there are times when you have to do things you would rather not do and things you don't like doing. It takes a strong person to embrace the task and get it completed.

I run a regular online event called the 10:10 challenge, where participants are encouraged to get up at 5 am for ten days to get a ton of things done for their business. Every day I am live in the group to set them the ten challenges and give them support and motivation.

It was day eight, and as usual I set a ten-minute timed task for the participants to do. I had decided to challenge them outside their comfort zone, so rather than a business task, I asked them to bake a cake. Yes, a group of businesspeople was asked to bake a cake, but before you shrug your shoulders and say I am barking mad, let me explain some more.

When I set the bake-it task in a 10:10 challenge, I honestly thought people would think it was a nice thing to do, but I was in for a shock. People were up in arms. They didn't like baking, didn't see the relevance, couldn't because they were away at a friend's house, and most claimed they didn't have time. Excuse after excuse not to bake a cake. How would you have reacted if I had set you a task to bake a cake in ten minutes?

The participants were showing their resistance to change and I got some strongly worded and irate posts. At first, I was gobsmacked at their reaction, but then I realised it was just highlighting the instant resistance so many of us feel when pushed outside our comfort zone. 'Cake Gate' was never about the cake. It was never about the amount of time I'd given the participants to bake it. It was about showing up the vulnerability of the mind. When faced with something different or difficult, our brains are quick to throw up excuses as to why we can't do it.

In reality, baking a cake in ten minutes is a simple task, but only a handful on the challenge looked at it logically. First, it had to be done. The next obvious step was to look into how to make a cake in ten minutes. A quick Google search would have shown the participants that there are hundreds of mug cakes they could make in under three minutes. Time challenge solved. Finally, it was time for the participants to make it a priority and fit those three minutes into the 1,440 minutes that we all have every day.

The people who embraced the challenge showed real grit. One person was staying at a friend's house, but still managed to make a mug cake using ingredients from their friend's cupboards. Another person made a proper cake, which was baked and iced by 7.30 am. Instead of people hating the challenge, they were reporting back how much they loved it.

The huge learning from this for everyone was that any challenge just needs them to think clearly, without emotion and drama, and logically work out how to get the task done. It was never about the cake; it was about the process and learning that it is easier to get something done when you take away the drama and excuses and just get on with it.

What can you learn from this? You will get challenges in life and business that are far greater than baking a cake, but when you lose the drama, lose the excuses, then the way to get the task done becomes clear. Don't let yourself have Cake Gate drama.

Get over yourself

Have you ever said, 'I want more people to know me', but in the next breath said that you don't want to be seen in your business? These two statements don't match. If you want to attract more clients into your business, you need to get yourself known, and that means fronting your business.

The thought of doing this may bring up limiting beliefs of not being good enough. I hear it over and over again. Therapists want more clients, but dread being seen and heard on social media or at networking events. Straight-talking alert – if this describes you, it's time to get over yourself.

You have a business where you see clients, and they quite literally 'see' you too. They see and hear you and buy into what you have, so why insist on shutting down to doing things like talks, videos, lives etc just because you dread what people will think of you? Sometimes the realisation that people are already seeing you can be enough to help you move forward and step up to the challenge.

I often joke with clients who say they don't want to be seen or heard when marketing their business. My reaction is to point out that unless their current clients are coming in with headphones so they can't hear them and paper bags over their heads so they can't see them, then they have nothing to worry about. If you think like this, be aware that it's a limiting belief that is all made up in your head.

So many of us are self-critical of how we look and sound. Imagine you are being shown a photo of a large group of people, all lined up and smiling as a memento of a special occasion. You are in that photo too. It is a lovely picture of everyone, but the likelihood is that you scan it to find yourself. You skip past everyone else as they look lovely and focus on you.

The next thing you do is criticise what you look like, how you are standing, the fact you look larger than you thought you were. But unless you were stepping out of line in the photo, running around the front naked, you will be the only one who is critical of how you look. How do I know? Because everyone else in the picture is likely to be doing the same thing as you, only criticising themselves.

Step outside your comfort zone for your business. If you want more clients, then you have to do things that make you feel a little uncomfortable, but if you really think other people care what you look and sound like, it's time to look at your limiting beliefs. Your current clients never complain, so why would anyone else who sees your marketing be any different?

CHALLENGE - BE SEEN!

Take a different mindset to fronting your business by realising it is just a limiting belief that is holding you back. No one minds how you look or sound. Instead of worrying about what you perceive others will think, step outside your comfort zone and allow yourself to be seen. Getting known will pull in more clients, but hiding and wishing won't.

5

Understand How – Customer Care

What exactly is marketing?

The *Oxford English Dictionary* defines marketing as:

> 'The action or business of promoting and selling products or services, including market research and advertising.'

Not very inspiring, is it?

At one of my live business training events aimed at helping therapists get more clients, the room was filling up with business owners. One of the delegates arrived early and asked, 'Will you be talking about marketing today?'

I was totally floored by this question. It was the first time I'd realised that many therapy business owners thought of marketing as one part of a business – a part they didn't like or want to do. A singular targeted action that was necessary to promote a business. This question surprised me as I thought it was obvious I would be speaking about growing a healthy business, and to me, marketing is *everything* about business. It is *not* just about putting out adverts and running promotional events. This is an important point to remember.

Marketing starts from the day you imagine what your business will be like, when you tell family and friends what your ideas are. It continues when you plan and create the business you want, when you get your first client, and carries on for the entire life of your business. Everything you do will have a marketing effect.

Marketing is much more than just promoting your work or product. It's how you show up, how you are perceived, the presentation of your clinic, how quickly your website loads, how polite you are on the phone, how easy it is to book an appointment. Customer care, professionalism and empathy are key to your marketing success. Yes, it's good to have a plan that guides you through the usual forms of traditional marketing, but remember that word-of-mouth marketing will usually outstrip any other type. If you create excellent customer care (that costs nothing) by treating your clients well, overserving and supporting them, this is better than any sales campaign.

Marketing methods can enhance your business, but please don't separate them from excellent customer care. You need both, and you need to be persistent and consistent. Unless you make sure everything you do in your business is excellent, you will struggle to make it grow.

This is why the fourth of my five principles, understand how, is such a huge subject. It's all about knowing the nuts-and-bolts marketing for your business, so there is no way I could fit it into one chapter. Instead, we'll look at excellent customer care in this chapter, then we'll cover becoming the go-to expert in Chapter 6, getting creative in Chapter 7 and keeping it going in Chapter 8.

Sleazy, heavy-handed sales don't work

Marketing has changed, thank goodness. People are fed up with heavy-handed sales techniques, and it's likely you hate selling in that way. Instead, potential clients are looking for ease of booking, a personable and knowledgeable therapist, and a service that is nothing short of excellent. The public have got wise to marketing methods involving lies, trickery and, let's face it, unethical tactics, so don't be tempted by any 'get rich quick' promises.

I am always encouraging people to be real when they do their marketing and I will continue to do so. You will often hear the word 'authentic' bandied about, but are you really being authentic? Being you means there is no competition; just you sharing yourself for others to connect with.

Get your head around being true to who you are in your marketing. Your current clients buy into you due to your skills, but even more, they buy into your unique personality. You can be the best practitioner in the world, but if you are rude and lack people skills, you will struggle. The combination of professionalism, empathy and personality is the real essence of your success.

I have noticed an increasing trend for people to post things that they say are from the heart, but honestly, they are not fooling anyone. Stiff, formal, overrehearsed, heavily scripted, uncomfortable – I even saw someone's post that was a complete copy of the coach that they followed. Being you is about just that: being you. You need to show up as your best self. It's obvious you don't want to be down, moody or in a strop; be the you who is professional, empathetic, kind, caring, enthusiastic and, of course, knowledgeable in your area of expertise. Be the human voice behind your business. People like you to be professional, but they also like to learn about you and what you do.

Marketing is about people getting to know you and learning about your skills and expertise. Keep your shared content simple rather than trying to impress your peers. Remember you are not selling to your peers, so don't let your ego get in the way. Clients will love it if you share tips and advice to help them. You will then be positioning yourself as the go-to expert, as well as being totally real and likeable. This is the best way for people to automatically want to buy into you and your services, creating a lifelong connection and recurring business model.

I remember an afternoon when I was sitting outside a café with my daughter, enjoying a drink in the shade. Across the road, we could see a skincare shop that was actively touting for business. Two salesmen with very different approaches were standing in the doorway.

The first was waving free samples at the people walking by. People reached out for the free sample just as it was drawn away from them, like a carrot on a stick. The passers-by stepped in closer to take the offer, but once again it was withdrawn. The salesperson then walked backwards, waving the sample while gesturing for the passers-by to come into the shop. They were never given the sample.

The second salesman had the same sample and was actively giving them to passers-by. This was the first contact the passers-by had with him and he'd gained their trust from the start. His offer was real. He then smiled and engaged the passers-by in conversation about several things for five to ten minutes. Finally, he invited them into the store.

The two salesmen were selling the same product from the same shop, using the same giveaway. Both were similar in looks and build, but the second one was successful with every person he spoke to. The first one just made people angry at the false promise of a giveaway, which he never once gave out. He didn't get one person into that shop.

This is a great example of people buying people. They don't want sales gimmicks or false promises.

CHALLENGE – MAKE TIME TO CHAT

Take the time to chat to clients and potential clients on subjects other than what you are selling. This is how marketing works for all of us today. Be kind. Don't jump in with heavy sales techniques; instead, engage, be empathetic and share as much helpful information as you can.

Sit, wait and hope marketing

Sit, wait and hope is the marketing method that I used to use, and one that many therapist business owners still hope may work for them. Here is a scenario that you may recognise:

You arrive at work for a 9.30 am client. When you have seen them, you write your notes up and tidy around. Then you sit and read for a while, text a friend, spend time on YouTube watching cat videos, waiting for the phone to ring, waiting for another client to appear needing your services. But the phone doesn't ring. You wish you were busier like other therapists you know. You wish you could be more like them. You hope that your day will change. Surely the phone will ring? Surely someone walking past will know to come in?

You lock up later that afternoon with a small amount of cash in your hand, but only one patient all day, reassuring yourself that tomorrow the sit, wait and hope method will work. Well, you hope it will! After all, when you qualified, you thought that clients would be beating a path to your door.

Here is the truth about running your own business. When you work for yourself, you have to find self-motivation and drive. I am not saying you have to be the Duracell Bunny on overdrive (as I can be), but you must be motivated enough to take some action for your business. Sit, wait and hope is *not* a marketing method. Although you may get a small trickle of clients, it is never going to build the business you want.

If you want change, you have to make it happen. Make a pact with yourself to think positively. Give up on your excuses; if you want success, you are going to have to make it happen. Plan, make long-term goals. Take short-term actions, but commit for the long term. Be persistent, consistent, and most of all, enjoy the journey. Remember, as Arthur Ashe said:

'Success is a journey, not a destination.'

Excellent customer care

Bad customer care is one of my biggest bugbears. My kids cringe when I am in shops and restaurants and the customer care is poor; it makes my blood boil. Taking good care of customers is essential for the success of any business and implementing it is simple, and it's free. It is harder to be rude and give poor service than it is to give excellent customer care.

Make sure that you show up as your excellent self 100% of the time. If you have a team around you, ensure that they do so too. I get so frustrated when I see staff who are miserable, refuse to make eye contact or look inconvenienced when asked a question.

My clinic has won many awards, but I am most proud of the customer-care awards. Think about it – isn't that why we all went into a caring profession? To give customers our care? Anyone who thinks customer care is not important when growing a client list is very much mistaken and missing out on an essential and powerful piece of free marketing.

Customer-care plan

Excellent customer care is anything that makes your customers feel welcome, feel valued and want to return to you again and again. Do it well and they will become your own mini marketers as they sing your praises to their family and friends.

CHALLENGE - YOUR CUSTOMER SERVICE PLAN

Take some time to think about your last shopping experience. Was it enjoyable or did you get agitated by the person serving you? The easiest way to work out what you want in your customer service plan is to start with what you don't want. Take notice of the customer service you receive wherever you go. What made you frustrated, angry, sad? List everything down, and then work out how you can do things differently. How can you make sure your customer service is nothing other than excellent?

When you're providing customer care, good is just not good enough. Remember that your business is all about you. You are the essence of your business. People buy into who you are, how you come across and how well you treat your customers. Do it well and you will attract new customers; do it badly and you will repel the ones you have.

There is no option to have a bad day. Clients come to you expecting the same excellent customer service time after time. If things are really going badly in life outside your business (eg a relationship split or the death of a loved one), acknowledge that you cannot be at your best, book some time off, and get back to work when you know you can be excellent. You are the therapist providing a service, so no client wants to hear your problems, gripes or moans when they come to see you, no matter what. Don't make their treatment session all about you, and never be miserable and grumpy with them.

It is important to set out your customer-care plan, whether you are a sole practitioner or have a larger premises with multiple staff. If you work alone, you have full control of this, but if you have staff and other associates, you will need to make sure everyone is working to the same high standards. Regular training sessions to guide staff on your standards of customer care are vital if you want to grow and retain your client numbers. Make sure everyone knows that it is a priority, not just if they feel like it.

What do you include in a customer-care plan? You could ensure that you and all your staff have a standard greeting for clients. Ensure you make eye contact and everyone is welcoming to anyone entering your clinic. How difficult would it be to offer someone a cup of tea if they arrive early or are waiting for a relative? It's often the little things that make the biggest difference. Set out that you and your staff will listen to any questions clients ask and respond politely. If you don't know the answer, make sure you have a procedure to follow. For example, reception staff could take the client's name and number so a therapist can call them back asap.

Include in your plan what to do if you get a complaint. Make sure everyone knows how quickly to respond and in what format. I will talk about complaints later in this chapter, so all I'll say here is to be prepared for them. Even though your job is to avoid getting them as much as possible, they will come. If you have a planned process to follow, it is likely to ease the severity of any complaint. Set out in your customer-care plan guidelines for everyone at your clinic, including your mum if she answers the telephone for you occasionally.

It is imperative when you employ someone to front your business, eg reception staff, that you take your time assessing their application and at the interview process. Taking references is another essential. The same is true if you need to take on more therapists or associates. Make sure you find people who will embrace your customer care. I never take anyone on, despite the level of their qualifications, if they don't come across as personable and likeable.

How to implement your customer care

Working for yourself from home

In this case, you *are* the customer care, so in theory implementing the right level of care should be easier than it is for those employing staff and associates. You do need to take a long, hard look at yourself, though, or perhaps ask for feedback from family and friends with regard to your customer care.

Always look to improve on what are you are currently doing. Working from home can be convenient, but remember to keep the area you use for work as professional as you can. The last thing a client wants is to walk past your washing pile, hear your dog barking or your kids screaming, or see your household clutter. Make sure, if it is possible, that you keep your treatment area completely separate from your living areas. If you are not able to keep it separate, then keep the parts of your house that clients access tidy and clutter free at all times. If you are using your living room as a waiting area, clear as much personal stuff out of the room as you can, and do exactly the same if you have a dual purpose for your treatment room.

Make booking appointments a simple procedure. If you have someone who will answer the phones for you while you are busy, that is ideal, or you could use a virtual phone answering service. It is not a good idea to have a phone line that can be randomly answered by children or family members who may not always be professional. To avoid this, you could get a separate number for clients to call to ensure the phone will always be answered professionally, or train family how to answer.

Whatever phone line option you choose, make sure that if you are not available, you set a message on your answerphone to advise people when you will be free to call them back. This may have to be changed on a daily basis, but I promise you will retain more clients if they know you will get back to them. If you don't inform clients clearly, it is likely they will move on to the next contact number they have on their list and book with someone else. Online booking is another great method to provide an easy experience. Make sure you set it up clearly and that it is simple and not glitchy to use.

Excellent customer care for your clients if you work alone would be to get cover when you take longer holidays, either a locum who will work for you or an arrangement with a local practice to see any emergency clients while you are away.

Working as an associate or renting a room

When you're working as an associate or renting a room, customer care gets a little harder as you are not in direct control of the clinic staff you work with. The simplest thing to do is to make sure you set up in a clinic that already has excellent customer care.

When you go to look around a clinic, remember that you are vetting the owners and other employees as much as they are interviewing you. What does the clinic feel like? Do you get a good first impression from the receptionist and other practitioners? Do the owners seem more interested in getting the rent for the room than knowing about you and what you do and your experience? Does anyone mention a clinic ethos or how they like to do things? If not, then ask those questions of them.

If you are already working in a clinic as an associate or if you are renting a room, then you need to be your own advert for customer care. Lead by example as it may well rub off on others, especially if your diary is continually full and others have empty slots.

What do I mean by leading by example? Make sure you leave any worries, upsets and anxieties at home. Being a therapist is about your expertise, but it is also about performance and no one wants a miserable therapist, no matter how bad you are feeling.

Running a multi-practitioner clinic

Employ the right staff to help promote your ethos of excellent customer care. I have always had a great team around me and I am under no illusions that my clinic business would have been so successful without them. If you are taking on self-employed therapists, the same principle applies: vet them carefully before they start working in your premises. When you're taking on staff and associates, make sure they have all agreed to implementing your plans and want to be part of a team. Too many times I see associates joining clinics with little or no interest apart from the taking of their commission. You are best to avoid this type of therapist if you want to grow your practice.

It is imperative that you lead from the front. If you present yourself as a professional who always has time for clients and your team, then those around you will follow suit. Carry out regular staff training to ensure you keep your standards high. It is easy for staff to become complacent, so regular training checks ensure that procedures are being followed.

Make sure you are visible in your clinic and interact with all your team members. It is your job to build good morale. Being constantly hidden in a treatment room, never investing time in your team, is poor people management, and your business will feel the effects.

CHALLENGE – TREAT EVERYONE WITH RESPECT

Treat everyone with the respect they deserve, which means being courteous to everyone and valuing them as human beings. Sounds such an obvious thing to say, but believe me, I have seen some therapists who treat clients with less than favourable customer care. Clients will talk about you, so make sure it's in a way you would want.

Complaints

Obviously, as a therapist, you want to work hard to make sure all your clients are content and happy with their treatments. You strive to do your best at all times. You are professional, you exude excellence in what you do, you gain informed consent, explain any risk and consider client modesty where appropriate. You may do all these things, but please believe me, a complaint can come from anywhere, and usually when you are least expecting it. Would you know what to do?

The best way to handle any type of complaint is to be prepared. Make sure you have a procedure for handling it. Getting a complaint is stressful and it may be that you wouldn't behave as rationally as you should. Setting out a structure before it occurs has it covered without drama or making things worse.

Here are my top tips on being prepared:

1. Try to avoid complaints. Be a true professional at all times. Make sure you communicate your treatment to clients before you begin. Gain the client's informed consent by making sure they really understand what is involved, checking regularly throughout the treatment that the client is still consenting. Explain clearly any risks involved with treatment, and please don't forget client modesty. Use towels and robes if you are a manual therapist.

2. Set out a clear complaints procedure. Write out the stages of action you will take if you receive a complaint, and make sure the client knows what to do and whom they need to contact too. Display a notice in your clinic/waiting room to notify them.

If you are in a regulated profession, make sure you give your clients details of how to contact your regulating body directly if they wish to do so. In another document, set out your own actions step by step, for example how long you will take to reply or acknowledge receipt of the complaint.

3. Respond fast. This may only be to acknowledge receipt of the complaint, but there is nothing more likely to exacerbate a complaint than no response. Do not bury your head in the sand.

4. Respond in a rational manner. It can be easy to lose your temper or feel a complaint is unjust, but please do not reply with these thoughts at the forefront of your mind. Instead, sit down and draft a reply. Ask someone to look at it for you, and definitely don't send it by return. Instead, wait a few hours and reread it. Can you remove any of the emotion that you were feeling? If you respond with an attacking reply, again, this will do nothing but fuel the complaint.

5. Refund. You can offer a refund as a gesture of goodwill, and sometimes that will be the best resolution.

6. Assess how serious the complaint is. If a complaint is of a serious nature, then contact your insurance company for advice as soon as possible. You can acknowledge receipt of the complaint, but don't respond any other way until you have taken legal advice.

Above all, be prepared, and never reply in anger or with emotion. Instead, remain professional and non-judgemental. If you can sort out the problem then do so, but you must remain calm and professional. Drama will just fuel the fire you are trying to extinguish.

How to avoid complaints

For about six years, I sat on the investigating committee for my governing body, and my role was to make rationalised decisions on whether a complaint needed referring on for further investigations. After reading many complaint reports, I noticed that often it was poor communication that led to complaints being made in the first place.

Poor communication may not always lead to an official complaint, but it can mean a client will not return, and they certainly won't recommend you to others, so good communication is an essential part of your customer care. Make sure you explain everything clearly to your client.

When making bookings:

- Make sure you repeat the time and date and check the client knows where the clinic is

- Make sure the client is aware of your charges

- If you need the client to bring anything with them, advise them

- Let the client know if they may be asked to undress

- Tell them how long the appointment will be

When the client comes to the clinic:

- Spend a few minutes explaining who you are and what you will be doing. You have from a tenth of a second to seven seconds to make a first impression, so make it a good one.

- Gain consent from the client for the treatment before starting and throughout treatment. This can be verbal or written, but I prefer to do both.

- Make sure the client feels comfortable. This could include providing pillows, an appropriate room temperature, decent lighting and covering their modesty with towels if you are a manual therapist.

- After a treatment, explain clearly any aftercare and advice, and any aftereffects they may experience.

Never underestimate the importance of customer care. You need to aim for excellence at all times. Customer care is free, it is easy to do with some planning and training of staff, and it is the best marketing tool you can ever use, so sit down now and plan your strategy. You will be amazed at the difference it makes to your business.

6

Understand How – Become The Go-To Expert

Your business relies on you. You are the person who needs to step up, step out of your comfort zone and get it on the map, and one of the key things in marketing your business is to get yourself known as the go-to expert. The person people talk about when they're giving recommendations to friends. The expert people know they can come to for help in your specific area. The professional, empathetic, kind therapist who will give them the very best.

But how do you get that status? Well, it doesn't come with sitting, waiting and hoping.

There are many reasons why people avoid pushing themselves forward in their business, but you will only see a change if you make a change. If you are not ready to step outside your comfort zone, you will never know what you could have achieved. I love the poem 'Better To Try And Fail Than Never To Try At All' by William F O'Brien, in particular this line:

> 'Life can be lived either way, but for me,
> I'd rather try and fail, than never try at all, you see.'

Not trying doesn't make sense; in fact, it means you have failed already. Be the person who tries as you will likely be amazed at the results. Hiding yourself will never benefit your business. I am not saying you need to boast, brag or force people into becoming clients, but you do need to show that you are the expert by sharing, informing and educating them about you and your therapy with great tips and advice. Get out to networking events; give talks to local clubs and businesses; tell friends, family and neighbours. Get known in your local community by helping out, supporting groups and generally becoming liked.

Word-of-mouth marketing

Word of mouth is one of the best and most effective methods of marketing. Consumers are shunning old-fashioned marketing techniques by scrolling straight past alerts on social media and fast forwarding adverts on TV, throwing direct mail straight into the recycling and unsubscribing from emailing lists.

Clients love to tell their friends, family, work colleagues etc all about a good product or service. They enjoy helping people they know by telling them where the best place to go is. Word of mouth influences people's decisions to buy. It will bring you customers who are already sold on what you do and feel confident visiting you. Customers who are brought to your business via word of mouth are more likely to talk about you after their experience than those who were referred by other means. Don't underestimate the power of word-of-mouth marketing for the success of your business.

To get good word-of-mouth recommendations, you need to attract an army of raving fans to your business. Fans who will want to tell their family and friends about you and what you do. You need to become the go-to expert. To do this, make sure you are always professional while remaining friendly and approachable. Overserve your customers with excellence in your particular area of expertise. Know your limitations of practice and refer if necessary. Be safe and get consent for what you are doing at all times; don't assume someone is OK. Consent and communication are key elements of gaining good word of mouth.

Be welcoming and helpful to all clients. You will get the occasional 'difficult' client, but over the years I have enjoyed treating them as I like the challenge of showing them how nice I can be, and many are now among my favourite clients. Clients who seem difficult have often got other issues going on, and as a therapist, part of your job is to recognise this and incorporate empathy into your treatment plans. You will get nowhere by responding to a difficult client with anger or annoyance; instead, defuse the situation with kindness.

Remember that the largest amount of referrals will come from clients, and how you come across will get you those referrals as much as your excellent treatment. Clients are brilliant at spreading the word about a good therapist, but they can also give negative feedback to their friends and family when their experience is not so good. Doing simple things like offering a drink to someone who is waiting or taking a client's wet coat and hanging it somewhere to dry is enough to impress a client. Don't underestimate the power of the smallest act of kindness. It costs you nothing, but the effects are huge.

Everything about your business, from the ambiance and customer care to the treatment you give, will have an effect on whether clients walk away wanting to tell all their friends about their experience.

Bad word of mouth

I have spoken about good word of mouth, but please be aware that you can attract bad word of mouth if you're not careful. This is something you want to avoid at all costs as it can be the fastest killer of any business. People like to spread good word of mouth, but they will spread the bad stuff even further.

Think back to a good customer-care experience you had – did you tell many people? It's likely you did, but only a handful. Now think back to a bad customer-care experience – did you tell many people? Chances are you told anyone who would listen. Your clients are likely to be the same.

What should you do if you get some bad word of mouth about your business? Definitely don't ignore it. Instead, contact the person and politely ask how you can do things better. Give them a chance to tell you what they felt went wrong and respond in a positive way. Never respond in an angry way, even if you believe what has been said is untrue. Responding in anger is likely to come back and bite you ten times harder. Be the adult and respond in a polite and helpful way.

A good, kind and helpful response to perceived poor service from your business can turn out to be a good marketing method in itself. Aim to understand your customer's point of view and offer help and a resolution to the situation. Remember, no drama.

Good word of mouth is what you are looking for, so be excellent! Giving the very best service you can all of the time will ensure you avoid bad word of mouth. Monitor what people are saying about your business, both good and bad, and respond accordingly. Track your customer experience by regularly asking for feedback and making necessary changes.

Social media

These days, most people have heard of social media, but often it can seem confusing, and many therapists are unsure of how to use it to promote their business. Some are actually repelled by it. If that's you, it's time for a reality check and a different perspective on what social media actually is.

Social media is just that. It is a place to be social, and if you are ethical and professional when you use it, it is never going to ruin your life, take over your world or harm you in anyway. As humans, we like to be social. We used to send letters, read magazines and phone people up for long chats. Social media lets us do all that in a space that can be worldwide, if we wish it to be.

If you don't currently like social media, please rethink your beliefs on it as it is important to see how it can help your business rather than hinder it. Social media does not control you; you control it, and the majority of the social media platforms are free for personal and business use. What other marketing systems do you know that offer their services free? Never before has there been a no-cost way to market your business with such reach.

Social media gives you a platform to engage and share information with your potential audience. There are many social media platforms, but right now Facebook is the biggest. This platform has billions of users and is still growing. It is ever changing, but keeps community at the heart of its focus.

Keep ahead of what social media platform serves your potential clients best. Where are they hanging out? That is where you should be hanging out too. It can be tempting to start up accounts for your business on three or four different social media platforms, but my advice would be to pick one and to do it well. There is nothing worse than a business owner starting many accounts for their business, but giving up on all of them after a few months.

Let's look at setting up a business account on Facebook as an example. If you have a private Facebook account, from there it's easy to set up a business page. If you don't, Google how to set one up and get it done. Don't run your business from a personal page as you won't get access to the business insights, and Facebook could shut you down. Google is a wonderful thing and all the answers to setting up are there for you to find and action.

You social media needs to be branded, just like you would brand your website (we'll cover branding in more detail in the next chapter). Let any customers visiting your profile know who you are by the consistency of your branding. Make sure you have good, clear graphics for your header banner and a great profile picture. People really want to know what you look like, so don't hold back on this.

Fill in as much as you can on your social media bio, including a link to your website, details on your location and how customers can contact you. Don't be tempted to make your bio just about sales; instead, make it professional, but with personality too. Remember, you don't want to be talking sales the first time someone reads about you. Of course you can tell them what you do, but no hard and pushy sales.

A social media page is for reach – to reach new clients and serve those who buy into you already. There are some key things you can do to grow your audience and following on social media.

Posting regularly is a good way to raise your profile and get yourself known as the go-to expert. Social media is about showing up persistently and consistently for your audience. It will not work if you rock up for a few weeks, then let the tumbleweed take over your page while you ignore any interactions there. Social media only works if you put in the effort.

It is your job to create exciting and informative content. If you can make it entertaining and fun to watch, that is even better, but make sure it's helpful and share as much advice as you can. Remember you are creating content for your potential clients, not your peers, so focus purely on your clients and their needs. Simple is good, but never underestimate the power of your knowledge. You know far more than you may think you do, and what may seem obvious to you is usually the best type of information to share.

Share your own content. Write a short blog, upload a photo of you working or post a Facebook live. Remember that social media platforms love pictures, videos and lives, so make sure you create a variety to get the best from your page.

Avoid sending people away to look at other platforms (eg posting a link to YouTube from your Facebook page). Most social media are likely to penalise you for doing so as they want the viewers to stay on their platform. For example, they may not push your post out to so many people.

There are things you can do yourself to raise the numbers of people who see your posts, but the algorithms are constantly changing so keep ahead of what is new moving forward. Always post with a picture or video. Take courage and go live if the platform hosts that. This will get you more reach and you can have real-time interaction with your audience. Have a call to action with your posts, advising your audience what to do next. Do you want them to interact and leave comments by answering a question you have posted or book in for a free fifteen-minute chat session? Your call to action should be helpful, not a sleazy sales pitch. If you share enough stuff that is valuable to your audience, when you do post something more salesy, you will not offend and people are more likely to buy.

All social media platforms are about growing communities, and the best way to get more reach on your posts is to encourage interaction and comments. Create content that leaves the reader wanting to tell you how they feel or how helpful it was. Overserve your audience by providing tips and ideas.

Facebook group

A Facebook group is an area where you can invite people with similar interests. You may want to invite your current clients or a group of like-minded therapists to chat. You can also follow and join local Facebook groups and interact with the discussions, showing that you are an expert in your field. Do not hard sell in a group. Instead, gain the group's confidence by what you say and react to. If you do advertise in a group, make sure you read the terms or ask the administrator if they happy for you to post. It is always best to private message the group admin and ask if they mind before posting.

In a Facebook group, as with any social media, don't post anything you wouldn't want your mum to see. Don't post miserable and depressing things, bitching and moaning because others are doing it; be upbeat, friendly and informative. Always be the positive person in the group, not the sad sack who everyone wishes would leave. And above all, be you. Be the professional, caring and empathetic businessperson that you are.

The more you post content that is informative and welcoming, the more likely viewers are to convert to customers.

Get known in your community

Social media is an important part of your marketing, but don't forget that meeting real people face to face is also an essential part of getting known in your community as the go-to expert. You need to connect with people both online and offline.

There are huge advantages to getting known in your community. The more people know about you and what you do, the more they will talk about you and come to you when they are in need. Your community is full of people who are looking for someone just like you, but if you don't let them know you're there, they will go to someone else.

CHALLENGE – BECOME PART OF THE COMMUNITY

Take a look at your local community. Who have you got around you? Examples are local shops, traders, clubs, organisations and schools. There will be people who need/want your services, so now you need to make contact with them.

There are many ways to get known and one of the best is to volunteer. Actually become a part of the community. Offer your time to the local traders' association or an event. Remember you are not selling, you are getting yourself known. Give, give, give, and the calls for your services will come naturally.

I have listed a few more ways to get known as the go-to expert in your local community so that you can take some ideas away to put into action:

- Get known by local clubs. For example, offer all their members 10% off. This is a great way to get a foot in the door and it looks really generous. Or a faster route is to actually join a local club, but I would suggest that you only join one you would enjoy. There is no point joining the local tennis club if you have no desire or ability to play tennis.

Interact, be you and get known, with the added bonus of doing an activity you will enjoy in your spare time.

- Offer local schools raffle prizes for free treatments – this is a great way to have a presence at their events without having to pay a lot of money to market yourself in their brochures. You can also add the option for the winners to upgrade to a full treatment for a set fee as an add on.

- Ask your customers for reviews and testimonials that you can use (staying within advertising standards guidelines). If they say they are happy with your services and it's appropriate, ask them if they have anywhere they can show off your brochures or hand them out to friends.

- Take part in local events. For example, you could set up a stall at a village fete with a game for the kids and a free raffle for the parents (collecting GDPR-compliant data for future marketing campaigns). My practice takes part in Christmas events by turning the clinic into a grotto for the children. This is always popular and has got the clinic many new clients, but you don't have to have a large clinic to join in locally. This is the time to use your imagination (more on being creative in the next chapter). The more you take part in your community, the more people will get to know the real you. I promise it really does work.

Get known, get out there, give out and you will get back more. Things may not happen instantly, but the momentum will build, and eventually you will be known for great things both inside and outside of your clinic. A nice place to be.

Network effectively

Over the years, I have met a lot of people who have become great connections for my business, from photographers to experts in commercial lease negotiations. Many of those have also become friends and all are a huge part of my business success.

Networking both in person and online is a great way to get yourself known to potential clients as well as other businesspeople. Many therapists like to treat clients, but find it hard to make the transition to marketing and getting themselves out and about. But there are times in business where you need to be fearless; you need to get over yourself and realise that the sit, wait and hope method is never going to get you the income or client numbers you really want. If you want more clients, take action and develop a fearless attitude to networking.

One definition of fear is 'an unpleasant emotion caused by the threat of danger, pain, or harm'. Now come on, are you really fearful of going to a networking meeting and standing up to present who you are and what you do? Is it really going to cause you danger, pain or harm? Of course not, but I do know that fear can be irrational. Your fear could be that you will make yourself look like a fool, but that is unlikely. And the chances of actual harm befalling you are almost 0% (taking into account earthquake, fire or flood). I also know that fear can take hold of your physiology, causing a cascade of hormones, emotions and feelings as intense as if a lion was about to jump on you. Your sympathetic nervous system kicks in, and before you know it, you have a racing heart, sweaty palms and feel as sick as a dog.

To overcome the fear, you need a plan for networking. You need a structure and you need to remember it is not a matter of life or death. You also need to remember your why. Why do you want to attract more clients to your business? Is it to earn more money and take more holidays, or just that you love what you do and want to help more people? Either way, you need to get out that door, make people aware of what you do and show that you are the go-to expert.

Ever since I opened my first clinic many years ago, I have always done face-to-face networking. It can be hard to force myself out the door in the early hours, especially in the winter, and yes, it was hard initially to make small talk with people I didn't know, but I persevered. I regularly went to events where I could meet real people and I still see those initial connections as clients.

CHALLENGE - INVEST IN YOUR NETWORKING

To get started, find a meeting, sign up and pay in advance. You are far more likely to turn up if you have invested some money. Don't put yourself off by moaning that it is an early start (if you are doing a breakfast meet); instead, prepare well by going to bed an hour earlier than usual, setting out your clothes and getting your leaflets/cards into your bag the night before.

At a usual networking event, you will find a group of other small business owners, all looking to make connections. Over coffee, make polite small talk (nowadays I am the master of that) and gradually get to know people. Then there will often be a breakfast or dinner, depending on the time of day, and an opportunity for everyone to stand up and do a brief pitch about their business.

It is really important to get the best from your networking. Make sure you are approachable, kind and pleasant to be with. This may sound obvious, but I have been to many networking events where this is not always the case for all the delegates. Relax and be who you really are. Take time to listen to others and invite them to tell you what they do. Show a real interest in what they have to say. Work on building a connection and a rapport with them. Show up as the go-to expert, and if people do need your help and expertise, give advice rather than trying to make a sale.

Many networking events offer each attendee a slot to do a short talk about their business. This is usually a one-minute pitch, and is where you can differentiate yourself from others in the room and make an impact.

You may well be nervous, so start by clearly stating your name and your business – even if you're worried your mind may go blank, you're unlikely to forget your own name. Also finish with your name and business as that is what people will remember. During your minute, be different, but be you. Don't stand up and drone on about what you do and how good you are. Instead, add a bit of humour if you think you can carry it off (don't use it if not). Educate the attendees about your area of expertise or share some amazing facts. How can your tips and advice help them instantly? You could try getting them to interact with you, but don't force anyone. You could discuss the myths about therapy. Inform people that you are happy to chat afterwards if they wish to learn more.

At these types of events it is a good idea to have leaflets or business cards with you so you can swap your details with others if appropriate, but appreciate that it takes time to make connections when networking. And if you think that going to one networking meeting means the whole room of delegates will buy your services, you are very much mistaken. First, you need to build trust.

A good analogy is that if you went on a blind date, you wouldn't get down on one knee and propose that same day. In fact, you would probably date for many months before you even started thinking of wedding bells. Why then expect people to fall in love with you after one event?

My advice is to find local networking groups rather than larger national groups. Often the countrywide groups are expensive and may have rules that you have to attend every week. Some even ask that you make leads to others at each meeting, which can be stressful so is best avoided. Look at events run by organisations like your local chamber of commerce. These events tend to be cheaper and have less pressure on attending every week.

Google 'local networking groups' and see what comes up. You may be surprised what business groups you have around you.

CHALLENGE – MAKE CONNECTIONS

Time to get out of your clinic room and meet some real people. Yes, the one-minute presentation may make your stomach feel a bit queasy, but reality check – it is not going to kill you. Get a grip and make clear plans. Join a networking group local to you. Be you, make connections, and don't resort to heavy sales.

7

Understand How – Let's Get Creative

Brand your business

Branding is an essential part of building your therapy business. A common misconception is that branding is just a logo and leaflets, but it's far more than that. Branding expresses the essence of your business, portraying your ethos as well as your services. It communicates your values and shows clearly what your business stands for, encouraging people to buy into you. It needs to stick in people's minds so they associate your brand with excellent care and therapies.

Marketing may convince your potential clients to buy a particular product, but it is the brand that makes them want to buy that product for the rest of their lives. Think about companies like John Lewis, Apple and Virgin as great examples. Branding if done well will make your business stand out in the therapy world. It will be your unique identity.

There are three themes to branding:

1. Visual branding – logo, typography and colours

2. Brand voice – your tone and the language you use when talking to clients

3. Brand values – this is your clinic ethos, how you act and want to be perceived

Let's talk about a couple of famous brands as examples. Nike is actually named after the Greek goddess of victory, athletes and winners. The 'tick' the brand uses is supposed to represent the wings on which Nike flew down to earth to crown her winners, and you can easily see what values the company wants you to believe in. Sport and winning – a great concept for a sportswear company. Apple chose its logo to represent Newton's apple, which brings to mind discovery, innovation and forward thinking. This is just what Apple wants to be known for.

So how do you go about creating your own brand without spending a fortune?

• Write down your ethos for your clinic (see Chapter 3). What values do you want to portray and how will your clinic run?

- What is important for you?

- Decide on three to five core values

Examples of core values:

- Excellent customer care

- Integrated clinic care

- High-quality therapy

Now it's time to sort out the visual identity of your brand, eg logo, colours and typeface. You may recognise these traditional parts of the branding process. How will your logo and choice of colour and font translate what your therapy business is all about?

Colours are really interesting so I would suggest you do some research into them. You need to like the colours you choose, but make sure they fit your clinic ethos too. There are lots of websites that will help you choose your colours and give you the meaning behind them if you are doing it yourself. Google colours and see what you can pull up.

Once you have decided on your logo, colour and fonts, you then need to stick to them. All your branding, from business cards to social media posts, must look similar. Keep your brand consistent in whatever you do for your business. This way your brand becomes easily recognisable, and subliminally people will know it is connected with you.

Your brand voice is best described as your principles or tagline. For example, my tagline for Helen Bullen is 'Teaching, Business, Health' as it says what I do succinctly. You have a choice whether or not to have a tagline, but it is another way to get your branding recognised. Please, though, don't make it too cheesy.

All this information is great, but my strong advice here is to consider getting some professional help rather than doing your branding yourself and possibly ending up with a half-hearted and amateur result. A designer does this work all the time, so they have specialist programs and the artistic flare that will really set your business apart from others. Do some research on designers, look at their work, and if you like what they are doing, ask for a quote for the work you want done.

CHALLENGE – FIND THE PERFECT DESIGNER

A good designer will want to know all about you and ask you many questions. You want your branding to reflect you and your clinic's ethos, so don't feel pressured into accepting any designs you don't like. Take an expert's advice, but ultimately it is your choice.

Make sure anyone you work with includes any design changes in the price they quote as you are likely to want to tweak anything they create for you. If you are on a tight budget, outsourcing to designers on websites like www.peopleperhour.com and www.fiverr.co.uk can work well. Sites like www.canva.com are also useful for creating branded posters and social media posts for you.

If you already have branding that perhaps doesn't fit with your ethos, or maybe you just don't love it, then it is time to rebrand. Rebranding can give a real boost to a business, but it does need to be done carefully so get some professional advice first if you are unsure. Asking for personal recommendations is a good place to start.

Remember that branding is more than a logo, font or colour. It is the essence of your business and what you stand for. Enjoy your branding as it really can be a fun part of your business, and very exciting and rewarding when it is done well.

Website

We all realise that having a website is essential for a business, but over the last few years things have changed in the online world, and they will continue to do so.

When I started my first clinic many years ago, websites were only just appearing on the scene and I didn't know anyone who had one. A few years later, I decided I needed a website, but I had no idea what it was or what I needed in it. My partner works in IT (not websites) and he cobbled something together with a crappy cartoon of someone doing massage and some text. It was terrible and I didn't optimise it at all, so no one found it anyway. Now I think about it, thank goodness no one could find it!

Maybe you are too young to remember a time before 'online' was even invented, let alone used as a great marketing tool. Most of us use the internet at least once a day, and for many it is multiple times a day. We use search engines, with the most popular, Google, appearing in the dictionary now, so being visible on the internet is essential for any business. A website is not optional, but expected.

In the early years of websites, the buzz phrase was search engine optimisation (SEO), which was how you got your website to the top of the search rankings. These days, SEO is still important, but there is another beast that is growing called social media and content marketing. People now have more than one way to find a business, so it is important to know what direction internet trends are taking. And you need to be following them closely as they move fast. Remember that doing just one thing will not market your business.

Your website is your personal calling card. Think of it as an online brochure where people can find out as much or as little as they wish about you. It will help you get new clients and encourage others to return. You can use your website to increase your status as the go-to expert in what you do by informing and educating people about you and your business services.

Via a website, clients and potential clients have access to you twenty-four hours a day, seven days a week.

They expect a website to include your contact details so they can get in touch to book an appointment with you. Even better, you may have an online booking system they can use at any time.

There are key things you need to do to promote your website. These include having its uniform resource locator (URL) on any marketing material you give out. It is essential to make sure your website is compatible with any device your clients or potential clients use and that the graphics show in the correct format at all times. Make sure your website is fast to load and that pages are formatted. People are impatient, and if loading is slow, they will likely jump off your website and go to another. If you have an online booking system, make sure it is clear and easy to use.

The information on your website should be in a simple and clean format. Websites have moved on from text-rich *War and Peace* type forums. Instead, people want a website to look good, have great information but not overload, and above all be easy to navigate. It is essential that any landing page is clear and simple to read. Make sure your contact information is easily to hand; don't make it difficult for clients to find how to get in touch. Many people will only have jumped on to your website to find your contact details or directions to your clinic, so make sure they're clear and easily accessible.

Keep your website fresh and interesting with pictures and videos. You can ALT tag pictures (describe what each image is representing) so that Google recognises them to raise your website profile. Keywords also encourage Google and other search engines to know what your website is about, but please don't make it obvious that you have put keywords throughout your text, making it hard to read and likely boring. Google reviews can help the ranking of your website, so regularly ask clients to write reviews. Link your social media to your website too.

My preference is WordPress for setting up a website. I have personally chosen to pay a web designer, but I have also set up my own site using WordPress templates. The advantage of WordPress is that it is easy to make regular changes yourself. Always make sure that you can get into the 'back end' of your website (the area where you can update text and pictures etc). Some platforms for setting up your own website are written in Hypertext Markup Language (HTML) only, and that is difficult to understand unless you are trained. Google loves you to update your website regularly, so it is important to have easy access yourself as it will cut costs.

If you decide you need some help with building your website, you may employ an experienced designer. Make sure you get a fixed quote before they start work for you, and if you can, get two or three quotes to compare prices. Don't get caught paying £1,000s when you first set up and cash flow is low. Use your logical brain rather than your heart at this point and shop around.

To make sure you share content on your website regularly, include a blog and links to the feeds on your social media. Register your clinic with Google Maps and add that to your website so that clients can find directions easily. This also encourages Google to rank you more highly. Above all, keep your website up to date on a regular basis, and keep an eye on current trends in the look and content of websites. You need to keep evolving your website as the world of technology moves on in its trajectory. Things will change year on year, and you would be wise to keep up to speed with the way people interact online.

Content marketing

I love the fact that we have moved away from hard sell towards informing and educating potential clients. Thankfully the days of heavy sales and cold calling are over in the world of successful business owners (notice I said *successful*). The emphasis is on sharing your expert knowledge by providing interesting, informative and educational pieces of content for free. When people get to recognise who you are, what you stand for and how much you know, they will be far more likely to come to you for help as you will be the go-to expert in their mind. The sales will then look after themselves.

Content marketing describes anything you create to share valuable free content that's of interest to your audience. Its purpose is to educate and inform your prospective clients so that you attract them to become customers and repeat buyers. This may be simple to say, but I know a lot of business owners get really hung up on understanding how to write good content, what to write about and where to share it. I want to demystify it all and enable you to create effective content to increase your income without feeling like you are selling your soul.

First of all, it is important to think about who your clients are. Who are you targeting? Take a look at your current clients and work out some stats on their average age, gender, interests – anything that helps you identify who you are talking to in your content marketing. There is no need to be too specific, just get a general idea. This will enable you to make your content target specific. Aim to attract clients you enjoy working with.

Next, you need to think of subject areas that will interest, educate and entertain your target clients. The content you put out should be closely related to what you sell, so if you are a therapist, examples could be information about your therapy, what clients can expect when they visit your clinic and other information based around your expertise. The key to good content that will connect with your audience is to make it authentic and real, interesting and fun to read. Don't get too technical, as if you were speaking to your peers, but inform your audience in language they will understand and connect with. Speak from the heart, but beware of making claims that break advertising guidelines (see the Advertising Standards Authority (ASA) www.asa.org.uk). Create content that makes people see you as the go-to expert they like, trust and wish to do business with.

CHALLENGE - CREATE VALUABLE CONTENT

A good way to think about the content you create is to identify the concerns your clients have and give them clear answers to their questions. Create a story that they can relate to that may motivate them to phone and make an appointment with you.

Finally, you need to think about where you will post your content. There are many places that you can post, but you will need to be consistent and wait patiently for the returns.

The key thing to note is that when you write a piece of content, it is not for just one use. You can re-use it, resource it, cut it about and share in different ways, creating short posts, long posts, videos, talks. Utilise it as well as you can and in any way you can. Re-using content will save you a ton of time.

Getting people to believe in you and what you do takes time. One post on social media or one network meeting every six months is not going to have much effect on your business. We buy from people we trust and like, who we believe have the skills or product we need. The majority of your clients will either come from good word of mouth or because they have researched you. They may have read your blog, looked you up on your website, watched your video, met you at an event, liked what you do, and only then made a choice to work with you. It's rare that clients will call to book with your after just one touchpoint from your marketing. Instead, it is likely that they will need to see multiple marketing pieces from you and in different formats first.

CHALLENGE - BE REGULAR!

If you post your content sporadically, you won't gain any traction. Plan to send out your blog or newsletter regularly, and post daily on your social media. If you say you are going to do a talk at your clinic, show up and do it. Get to a networking event on a monthly basis. To get people to notice you and like what you do, you need to be consistent. Commit to taking action.

This may sound straightforward – all it needs is a bit of planning, but the key thing is to 'understand how' you are in this for the long term. Creating content is not just what you do for a few weeks after a training event or for a few months when you start up; it is a journey throughout the life of your business. You will not get traction from one post. You won't get huge traction from five posts, but if you keep at it, you will get traction and know that you are creating an audience of fans. Fans who will know to call you first when they need your services. Be helpful, be professional, be empathetic and keep showing up.

Attracting people to your content

Good content leads with a great title that attracts people to actually start reading. We are likely all time short, so content with pictures and videos attracts more attention as people can quickly work out what the post is about. Don't be afraid of using things like video for your posts. Good content doesn't have to be written; it can be in any form, and video will get you a wider reach. Vary what media your content is formed from. Write, film, talk, show, but make content consistently.

Please don't be the person who gives up and says, 'Creating content doesn't work.' Take a look at what you are doing and make sure you are doing enough. Make sure you are providing content that serves your audience, and most of all, remember once is never enough.

Ideally, with every piece of content you produce, include a call to action. Always tell your audience what to do next, whether that be how to contact you for a free fifteen-minute chat or how to get to your website to read more about you. It's not an instruction to 'come and buy', but rather it lets potential clients know how they can get even more help from you.

Believe in the process. You share helpful advice and tips, and before you know it, you will have positioned yourself as the go-to expert and the phone will start ringing.

CHALLENGE – WHO ARE YOU?

Create informative and interesting content that reveals who you are, including your interests and expertise. Focus on quality content that resonates with your audience, but add in some humour if it seems appropriate.

What to do if you hit a creative block

I create a lot of content on a regular basis and I take time out of my business to write it. I am fortunate that I have a creative mind that wakes me in the middle of the night, stops me in my tracks when I'm out running, and generally throws ideas about almost all the time. But on occasions, I do get writer's block, or 'creative block' as I prefer to call it – that feeling when nothing comes to mind, or you get an idea but you struggle to get things flowing.

For a lot of therapists, creating content is a difficult process, but there are things you can do to get your creative mind working. Start by writing about what you already know. This may seem obvious, but expressing things that you are passionate about will help the flow of your writing. Write about things that will help your clients, eg how to avoid injuries in the garden or information about a common condition that you see in your clinic. Be aware that you can be cursed by your vast amount of knowledge. It's easy to forget how much you actually know that other people don't, and you probably share tips and advice already with your clients without even realising it.

What do you say to your current clients when you're sharing advice with them? That can be great content, whether it is a simple stretch, a guide to hydration or any other tip you regularly give.

Always write down any ideas you get for content as soon as they come to you. Keep a content notebook or a notes section on your phone. Jot down ideas so that you can go back later and take them further.

Create titles from your ideas, as often a good title will trigger your creative flow. Other times, you will have to create the content before a good title reveals itself. We are all different. Remember content can be written, video, live, talk, so aim for variety.

CHALLENGE – LOOK FOR IDEAS

Ideas for content are all around you if you look out for them. Triggers for ideas can be pictures, news stories or local events. Think what help you can give to your clients. How can you educate and inform them?

Finally, watch what you claim. The ASA sets rules on what you can and can't say in your marketing, so you would be wise to stick to these rules. For more info, check out www.asa.org.uk

Create an active database

Creating a database is a good marketing tool for your business, but it must be up to date following the GDPR (General Data Protection Regulation) rules of 2018. Please check out www.ICO.org.uk for full rules and guidelines.

A database is a list of people who have agreed to receive marketing material from you. The emphasis is on *agreed*. So how do you collect a database?

1. For every new client, take all their personal details for your client file. An easy way to get details for your database is to take email addresses and ask the clients if they wish to receive your marketing material. Remember they must opt in rather than you signing them up automatically.

2. Have an opt in on your website where people who are visiting can sign up to your news/blog, again making sure they give you permission to put them on your database. You must be transparent about what you will be sending them, eg information and marketing.

3. If you attend events, you could have a sign-up form for clients, but again make sure you give them a choice to opt in to your database. A free raffle is a good way to do this.

Never share the data you have with anyone else. It is not good enough to have the information on a spreadsheet on your laptop; instead, it must be stored securely under GDPR rules. Make sure you have an easy unsubscribe option once people have signed up. Using a customer relationship management (CRM) system like MailChimp or Constant Contact will ensure your data is stored securely and will give you opt-out or unsubscribe buttons on anything you send out. An online CRM will also provide you with mailing templates.

Take some time to understand the data protection rules and watch out in case things change. You are responsible for your clients' data and need to act appropriately to keep within the law. Go to www. ICO.org.uk to read more.

It can be easy to get caught up in thinking that a database with hundreds or thousands on it is better than one with only a small number. The truth is, it is about quality, not quantity. Never buy lists of data. Firstly, they are likely to be against GDPR rules, and secondly, the people on them won't be your ideal clients. And no one likes their data being bought, so you could put off more clients than you gain.

Having a database is often a free way to connect with clients. I would recommend that you send out monthly news from your clinic; make it every other month if you really struggle for time. In your news, you can include relevant health topics, advertise new therapies or charity events, and offer money-off vouchers, for example. Keep your readers interested in what you do. Just like other types of content marketing, you need to help, inform and educate your audience via your news. Yes, you can advertise what you do, but don't make that the only reason you send out an email.

8
Understand How – Keep It Going

Track your marketing

You now understand how to market your business and you are taking effective action to get things done, but how do you know what is helping and what needs tweaking? It's all very well utilising a multitude of marketing techniques, but how do you know what is working for you unless you track it?

CHALLENGE – TRACK ALL YOUR TOUCHPOINTS

A mistake many business owners make is to do marketing but never track the results. Tracking your results will inform you as to what works for you, what marketing to rethink and what to repeat. Track how people first heard about you. Ask them to be specific.

> Create a tick list of all the places you do your marketing and encourage clients to fill in where they connected with you. They can tick more than one option if they connected through more than one of your marketing methods.

Your potential clients are likely to have had several touchpoints with you before they called in to see you. They may have heard about you from a friend or passed your clinic door. They may have then seen a post from you on social media. It's also likely that they took a quick look at your website. If you only ask them to tick one touchpoint, they are likely to tick the last one they used. Then you could think other marketing is not working. Get a true picture by asking for every touchpoint.

Once you get that feedback, you then need to take more effective action on the results. What marketing is working? Do more of it. What marketing is not proving fruitful? Make changes or scrap it. Remember also to get feedback from long-term clients. Ask about all aspects of your business, from ease of booking, customer care, your services, to the look of your clinic.

Feedback like this is essential to gauge what customers think of your business. Look at it rationally. Get anything sorted that seems to be a problem, and when you get awesome testimonials from satisfied customers, use them in your content marketing (remembering

that any testimonial has to conform to ASA guidelines
– www.asa.org.uk).

The lean times

Running out of cash is one of the main reasons new
businesses fold, and owning your own therapy business is no different. When you're planning to start up
a business, depending on the size of the business you
want, you would be wise to factor in some cash flow
to cover your initial costs. Unfortunately it is nearly
impossible to start your own business without some
back-up funds.

How do you go about getting your business started
and keeping it running in the early years of set up?
First you need to do some careful planning. What
are the costs of running your clinic going to be and
what will you need to earn to cover them each month?
Remember that the majority of therapy businesses, if
not all, do not make a profit in their first few months.
Some won't break even by the end of the first year, so
you need to plan for this. Being knowledgeable about
the flow of your cash is key.

When I started my clinic, I had a mortgage to pay, two
children I had to support on my own, as well as clinic
rental and costs. I needed to make sure that I had
enough cash flow to allow my business to flourish

and grow as well as cover all my costs. I didn't have a nest egg to rely on so I needed a regular income.

My decision was to do some part-time work elsewhere and I was fortunate to be offered some teaching work when I graduated, which I took willingly. And I didn't stop there; I also started working for the NHS as a rehabilitation support worker, which involved travelling around the local area helping elderly people get to bed. I was overqualified for this work, but I was prepared to do any type of job that meant I had enough income to support myself and my family while I set up.

Some therapists start their business while still in paid employment, which is another good way to ensure an income. The only word of warning I would give with this option is that sometimes therapists continue both doing their nine-to-five job and working in their therapy business for many years, and end up burning out. They also never get enough traction for their therapy business to be successful and financially supportive. Make sure you put a time limit on how long you will continue in your original job. Never jump ship before you should, but don't cling on to the comfort of your old job for too long either.

To help cash flow, watch your spending when you start up. It can be oh so tempting to have the latest gear and gadgets for your new clinic, but in the early stages, if it is not essential, you don't need it. As your business grows, you can always add to your clinic. Just get the basics to start with, build your income, and only then can you buy some of things you want rather than need.

CHALLENGE - REDUCE YOUR OUTGOINGS

This rule of thumb works for home expenses too. If you are serious about your business and getting it off the ground smoothly, then you may have to have a year or two of reduced expense at home. It's not the time to be buying the top-of-the-range car you have always wanted or to have multiple holidays. When I started, I didn't have an official holiday for over two years. It's the time to look at your outgoings and see where you can make savings. Check your bank account. Are you paying out direct debits on things you are not using? Go through your account carefully and cancel anything that is non-essential.

Cash flow is key to any successful business. You need to match what you want to happen in your business to your actions, and that includes saving and earning money.

Dream team

I put a lot of my success down to the dream team I have working for and with me at my clinic, but how did I get to have a team totally committed to both me and the clinic?

Before I opened the door to my multi-therapy clinic, I sat down and wrote a clinic ethos (see Chapter 3). It was really important to me that my team knew what I wanted and that we all sang off the same hymn sheet, and I had to tell them from the start rather than trying to implement what I wanted at a later date. Any new therapist or staff member who has joined since reads the clinic ethos, and if they disagree, they do not join the team.

To implement my clinic ethos, I led by example. I made sure that the clinic was a supportive environment for us all by being available for any therapist or member of staff should they need help. As a team, we often enjoy social events together, and I run regular training for staff and continual professional development for the associate therapists.

Another thing that I love to do is spend time working on reception each week. This allows me to see how my business is working on the frontline and highlights any difficulties my team may be having. The associate therapists know that I am around for them to talk through case scenarios that may be troubling them. This all means I now have a clinic of self-employed therapists and employed staff who are loyal to my clinic, its branding and ethos.

How do you go about getting the right people to work with you? The best way to find someone for your team is via word of mouth, eg another therapist knows them and sings their praises. I was 'lucky' (I use that word lightly) when I started out to be joined by graduates from my years of teaching and some of the osteopaths I had met while studying for four years (rather a long interview time). The majority of the other therapists I've taken on have come from recommendations, but I always suss them out myself first. I like to make sure that anyone who joins the team is a team player, so often I will ask a new therapist or staff member to join us at an outdoor event. Without them knowing, I watch how they interact with my team and with clients. It is surprising how quickly I can tell if they are going to fit in with the team and our ethos.

Obviously it is not always possible to take therapists to outdoor events, so another thing I do is ask them to come in for an informal interview with me and another member of my team, preferably two other members. After the interview, we all feed back on how we found the therapist, and this usually sorts out whether I take them on or not.

My top tip here is if you, or another member of your team, take an instant dislike to the therapist, then it is likely that some of your clients will feel the same. This may not seem fair, but often therapists only have a few seconds to make a client feel comfortable. I would also advise that you take self-employed associates on for a trial period of three months in the first instance. Once you know they are a good fit for your team, you can extend their terms.

For your reception, you need someone who can take some of the daily tasks away from you, and ideally you need a practice manager for that role. My practice manager is an absolute gem and I couldn't do without her. She has common sense and runs the practice like clockwork, taking a lot of the work away from me. But she also knows when to seek my advice.

Any reception staff I take on have to be pleasant, kind and have tons of empathy. They may not have great computer skills when they start, but that can be taught; being caring is harder to teach. Your receptionists are the lifeblood of your business, so please don't underestimate their role in the success of your clinic.

You are in charge of creating your dream team and communicating with them how you want your clinic to run. You must lead by example in your demeanour, customer care and professionalism. Put together the right team and your clinic will fly.

Competition

When I had my first clinic, working out of a room in a dental surgery, I was the 'only osteopath in the village'. I had an associate who worked for me and together we built up a healthy number of clients. Then the unthinkable happened... another osteopath decided to take on a retail unit right across the road!

I was so devastated, aghast and downright indignant that someone felt they could set up so close to me, I went to the council and logged my grievances against my competitor's change-of-use planning application and waited for a reply. The reply was not what I wanted. The council came back with a standard response about how planning was not based on whether there were other similar businesses in the area, but on things like parking issues, noise and disturbance. Much to my horror, the new clinic was set up across the road. It looked great and I was really worried.

My initial reaction was that this would ruin my business as I would stop getting new clients coming through the door. But what do you think happened? The exact opposite. My business continued to flourish and I felt no ill effects whatsoever from the new place opening across the road.

What I had forgotten to think about was that I already had a good clinic where I had become known for my skills as an osteopath and for excellent customer care. I was me and no one else could be me. I was good at what I did. In my blind panic, I had seen the other clinic as being better than mine and out to 'steal' all of 'my' clients. I had no idea what the other clinic was really like, but I knew I already had a good one, so why had I so quickly seen competition as a bad thing?

I learned that 'competition' is the wrong word to use for other therapists. We should all unite and work together. Instead of concentrating on your competition, focus on making your own clinic the best it can be. While it's good to know what others are promoting and their prices, it doesn't mean you have to drastically change what you do. Be confident in your ability and your set up. Work hard to promote yourself and to provide the best experience you can for clients, and the rest will sort itself. No one else can be you, and you need to be confident that you are good enough.

I'd like to finish the chapter – and indeed the 'understand how' principle – with a cautionary story. When I was first planning to start my large multi-healthcare clinic close to my home, I found the perfect premises behind the main village high street. It needed me to obtain change-of-use permission, but then I would be able to create a decent three-roomed clinic.

I put in my planning application to the local council and thought it would just be a matter of time before I got the notification that change-of-use had been granted. What I hadn't factored in was that the practice manager of another clinic down the road was on the warpath. She had taken the time to go around every business in the high street, portraying my proposed clinic as a busy surgery with appointments every ten minutes, which would cause congestion in the village. Before I knew it, my planning application had been turned down.

I was distraught and sat around for a few days, wallowing in self-pity, then I wandered into the village again. As I came down the high street, I noticed a 'To let' sign in the window of a large building. Fortunately, the estate agent was right next door, and within minutes I was inside the property. To my surprise and pleasure, the room I had seen was just one part of the commercial unit. Out the back it had a huge room that could be split into three treatment rooms, and the original room would be a beautiful reception area. At that point, I knew this would become my clinic.

Again, I had to apply for change-of-use, but this time I knew the process. At the same time as I set about filling in my planning application, I went and spoke personally to all the neighbours and local business owners, informing them what my clinic would be like. My planning went in, and yes, it was agreed.

All was well and I opened the doors in April 2010. You may think this is the end of this story, but here is what happened next. It appeared the practice manager of the other clinic was still on the warpath. The clinic changed its name to include multi-healthcare, just like mine. Then it changed its branding colours from blue to the green my clinic used and copied my adverts in a local magazine almost word for word. I was actually flattered, but it was weird behaviour. All the time I kept out of it and focused on delivering the best customer-care experience possible to clients.

One evening, I was in my clinic working late. It was June so it was still light outside, and from my desk I watched in amazement as a therapist from the other clinic got out of her car and calmly ripped down one of my posters. It was a deliberate decision and action.

What did I do next? I composed an email. I didn't rant, I didn't accuse; instead, I wrote and informed the therapist that I was concerned she had felt the need to pull down my posters and could she tell me what she found so offensive. Of course, I said I would be delighted to discuss it with her in person, but I never received a reply.

A few years later, that clinic closed its door. Because the practice manager and therapists had been so focused on the competition – me – they hadn't been focusing on what they could do for their clients. Meanwhile, I never got cross, I never responded in a negative way; instead, I focused on my clinic's journey without distraction.

Make sure you do the same.

9
Take Effective Action

You can know all the theories of marketing, but until you put them into action, your business will stay right where it is.

I know how easy it is to have good intentions to get things done. I know how easy it can be to feel motivated and inspired to really get your business on the map, but without some changes and action, that won't happen. Effective action is just that: action that is effective. You can be as busy as you like, but without the proper focus, it will only send you into overwhelm and frustration. You won't get the results you want, which can lead to you giving up. To be effective, you need to commit to actioning all the principles we have covered in this book. Don't skip any part or think that you just need to know a set of marketing methods and the results will come.

Let's get to the last part of this journey and talk about how you can stop being busy and take effective action instead.

Be persistent and consistent

Marketing your business is not something you do in a panic when things have gone a little quiet. Of course you can up your game if you feel you have down-times, but marketing is for the life of your business, and so is taking effective action.

Here is the mistake most business owners are making. They give up. They start full of hopes and ideas for their business, they try it for a week or perhaps even a month, and then they give up because they don't see instant results.

Marketing is a long-term activity. What you do today may gain results immediately if you happen to connect with someone who is in need of your service right now, but it's more likely to get results further down the line. I have had feedback from people who saw a video I had done some months ago, but didn't need my services then. Nonetheless, they kept watching what I was doing, realised I knew what I was talking about and that I seemed likeable and approachable, and when they did need a therapist, they knew exactly who to contact.

A lovely lady came to one of my one-day events. She had seen a live I'd done on a Monday, and by the Thursday had booked on to the event. *Wow*, I thought, *just one touchpoint and bam! She was in my world.*

It transpired that her signing up with me hadn't been quite that simple. This lady was a therapist who wanted to know more about marketing. Her sister, who had been made aware of my work during a chat with her neighbour, who had just happened to follow my Facebook page, had recommended she watch me on a video. Instead of one touchpoint, it was actually three or four (maybe more as I have no idea how many times the neighbour had watched me).

Never underestimate what you are doing or who is watching. It is not always the people shouting about you who get you the referrals and bookings. It can be something subtle, which is a good sign that you are sharing great content to inform and educate your audience.

The key to marketing is to know it is going to continue for the life of your business, so you must be consistent and persistent for the whole of that time.

Expect curveballs and wobbles

Life is a roller-coaster ride with ups and downs. Curveballs can come at us at any time as we follow its twisting and turning rails. They happen to us all, despite the best laid plans, but if we are not ready for those twists and turns, the curveballs can throw us off course and stop us in our tracks.

Being a business owner is great, but be prepared as there *will* be curveballs. The truth is, you will have times that test you in your life and your business, and if you want success, you will be well served to realise this. Your business needs you to stay focused through the difficult times. Don't let curveballs throw you off track; instead, pick up that curveball and throw it right back. Never let it stop you taking action.

Wobbles are also likely to creep up on you when you're running your business. Things like imposter syndrome and feelings of inadequacy can generally make it all seem a bit shit. But as you grow in confidence, those wobbles will get fewer and fewer. I confess I still get the wobbles, but thankfully they are rare these days.

A really cool thing you can do with a wobble is embrace it. Plan for your next wobble. How will you manage it? One of the best things you can do is down tools and get out for a walk. Listen to some motivational music, put on a podcast that you love, or just walk in silence. Do anything to break the wobble cycle.

Never wallow in a wobble, but you have full permission to rant and rave for five minutes to get it out of your system. Bawl if you want to, but get it done and dusted. Then cut the wobble and actively make changes.

When you're in the wobble state, you will never resolve the problem and it's likely it will just get worse. It is also likely to stop you taking action. Plan while you are in a non-wobble state (go and get a pen and paper now). What will you make sure you do when a wobble occurs?

For me, I allow myself a full-blown meltdown for five minutes, and let me tell you, I am the queen of meltdowns. Then once that's done, I smile. It is not a real smile initially, but the action of smiling kids your physiology. It doesn't know it's a post-wobble smile; instead, it thinks you are feeling good.

While I'm smiling, I sit and think of three things that I am grateful for. Then I get out the door. I run, I walk, but I get moving, whatever the weather. I choose to listen to up-tempo music or an inspiring podcast as I break the wobble cycle.

Next I return to take on whatever sent me into the wobble in the first place, and it's *always* easier to deal with when I have worked through my anti-wobble routine. Then I take huge action to resolve it, sort it out, make a change.

CHALLENGE – YOUR WOBBLE PLAN

What wobble plan will you come up with? Get it planned out now and write it on a sticky note to stick on your wall. Never wallow in a wobble.

Why are some people successful?

What is it that makes successful people different? It's not luck, so what is it? What do they do that makes them stand out? Most successful people share similar traits, but what are these traits and how can you emulate them to achieve your goals?

All the successful people I know or have read about have drive. Real, full-on drive. They work smarter than others on everything they do. I say smarter rather than harder deliberately as it can be easy to be busy, but not necessarily effective.

I am naturally highly driven and a lot of that comes from my competitive nature. I like to be the best, do the best. From my experience of playing top volleyball in my twenties and thirties, I know I want to win.

When I was a player, to be the best, I had to train regularly, be a good team member and have full-on drive to succeed. I also had to understand the tactics of the game. This experience has been great for me in my business too.

Here are some of the traits of successful people:

1. **They are willing to take risks.** Holding back will not help you reach your potential. Stepping outside your comfort zone may make you feel a bit queasy, but you have to take risks if you want to move forward. I am not talking huge risks like betting your house on your success, but do take calculated risks.

2. **They are willing to work.** Grit, hard work and motivation are essential. Being consistent and in it for the long game are what successful people are good at. They don't ever stop taking effective action.

3. **They admit when they are wrong.** No successful person will ever tell you they have never made a mistake. In fact, most will have tales of huge learning from things that went wrong. Admitting you are wrong then making changes is key to success.

4. **They know how to ask for help and delegate.** Those who are successful do the tasks they are good at and outsource those they are not. You can't be an expert in everything that happens in

your business and trying to will stop you building the business you want. Yes, you need to take effective action, but that could mean delegating parts of your business to others.

5. **Successful people believe they will be successful.** Not much more to add to this, except you need to focus on your own belief.

Outsourcing

There is no way you can be the expert in everything to do with your business, and my advice is you shouldn't try. In the beginning, when you start your business, you will probably need to do it all yourself, but when you get busier, your valuable time is better spent doing the things you are good at and enjoy.

Outsourcing certain jobs and tasks is key as you grow your business. Areas you are likely to want to out-source are accounts, design, reception, call answering etc. Of course, watch your budget, but remember that getting help with a task may cost you far less in terms of resources than the time and money you'll lose doing it yourself. Tasks where you lack knowledge can stop you in your tracks, so outsourcing can be an effective way to keep moving forward. Know your own expert-ise and spend your time on that.

If you need help with certain areas of your business, there are good places online such as www. peopleperhour.com and www.fiverr.co.uk. You can find anything from a virtual assistant to create your beautiful blog to a solicitor to help you draw up planning applications. These type of sites allow you to commission one-off jobs so that you are in control of your spend at all times.

Taking time out

It is so easy when you're self-employed to get completely wrapped up in working. You want to work hard, you want to succeed, and often in the early days you are doing the majority of the jobs yourself to save money. But did you realise that taking time out will give you clarity and make you more effective?

When I started my large clinic, I had a business coach for a few hours a month and I still remember his wise words about stopping and taking some time out, especially when I felt I had reached overload or I was stuck at a crossroads. He talked a lot about giving myself a virtual pat on the back from time to time, stopping and recognising where I had got to in my business and not just ploughing forward all the time.

Even a quick five-minute stop when things get too much can get you back on track. Your head will likely be telling you to keep going, but believe me, if you take a break, you will be more efficient when you go back to what you were doing. Taking time out can be done in many ways. It may be long term like a two-week holiday or short term like a half hour over lunch just to sit quietly, but whatever it is, it will make you more productive.

I personally like to go for a walk or a run, preferably in the countryside where I can enjoy great views to settle my mind and get clarity on problems. After I have taken some downtime, I always come back recharged. Normally my head has sorted out any problems, and I get creative when I take downtime so ideas just pop into my head.

CHALLENGE – FIND YOUR ESCAPE

You need to find your own escape. What makes you feel good? It may be cooking, reading or sitting quietly for a while. Just let your mind wander wherever it wants to go.

To really be effective, it is a good idea to schedule your time off. I have a rule that in general I do not work on a Sunday until the evening when I hop on to my social media for a while. When I feel myself getting stressed or overwhelmed, I get out for ten minutes. I go for a walk in the sun or just stop and sit to clear the fog in my head. Taking time off is also important so you can see your family and friends, as if you are not careful they can feel neglected.

Your to-do list

'Brain dump' is a lovely expression. For me it says exactly what it needs to do. A brain dump is time to get all the thoughts and ideas that are going round in your mind out of your head, as we discussed in Chapter 3. You can go back now and reread that section if you need a reminder.

Remember a brain dump is great for organising all your thoughts into a real action plan, whether it's for the whole of your business or for individual ideas and projects. Once you have done a brain dump, the next thing you need to do is to create a to-do list. I am not talking about a list that just gets longer and longer or a list of things you have already done so you can tick them off; I am talking about a working to-do list that will help you take effective action in the most time-efficient way.

A great way to organise a to-do list is to split it into specific areas. What:

- Will get you more clients and increase your income?

- Have you been avoiding?

- Needs to get done today – priority?

- Needs to be done this week?

- Can wait until next week / next month?

- Needs to go on your waiting list to look at in a few months?

To-do lists are a great way to keep all your to dos in one place, but they can become long and overwhelming. Then you don't know where to start and you stop before you have even begun.

Here is how to manage a to-do list. From your main list, create a list of things that need to be done today, eg paying your rent or employees' wages. Then drag across anything on your list that you have been avoiding (there will be something). Look at the task you are avoiding and make sure you have split it down into small enough sections. If the task is too big, you will be overwhelmed, so break it down. It will be much easier to manage and action.

A great way to keep a to-do list in order is to go over it at the end of the day. Tick things off that you have done and refresh your list for the following day. What is a priority, what have you avoided, etc? It saves a load of time if you can wake up and your to-do list is already planned.

Avoid procrastination

You have brain dumped and created a to-do list, so the next thing you need to do is to take effective action. But that is not always as easy as it sounds.

Procrastination is a monster that can rear its ugly head at any time, usually when you least expect it. You know you have a task that needs to be done, and yet you will do anything to delay and postpone it. I always know I am procrastinating when I start to fuss over getting another drink, finding another pen, doing other less important jobs. At my worst, I have even decided that the ironing is suddenly more important than the task I need to get done. Generally there is nothing that the ironing outranks, which shows how illogical my brain is when I am in full procrastination mode.

The key to managing procrastination is to recognise it. If you know what you are doing, it is easier to stop yourself.

There are many reasons for procrastination. Fear of failing is a common one, and the fear of what might happen becomes bigger than the fear of never getting started. In reality, you need to change your mindset. If you never start, how will you know what could have been?

Wanting things to be perfect can stop you getting things finished (or even started) and out into the world of your potential clients. This sort of procrastination is a hard one to manage, but please understand that nothing will ever be perfect, so why wait until it is? You will have a long wait. Setting timed targets can help counteract the need for perfection, but you do need to stick to the planned target time.

Another common cause of procrastination is a lack of focus or perceived lack of knowledge. In these instances, it is important to make any task simple enough to do. Break it down into easy bite-size pieces. Get help on anything that you don't understand by asking someone or researching it. Google and YouTube are useful for this.

Timed tasks

I use timed tasks when I need to be productive and make sure I get things done, especially with tasks on my to-do list. To make a timed task work, you first need to ignore the procrastination voice in your head. No listening to it telling you that something is more important or you don't have time or you fear failure. Instead, turn off all distractions like emails, messages etc, then set a timer to run for ten minutes. The world will not collapse because you are focused on one thing for ten minutes, but I assure you, you will get more done than you may have ever expected. When I run my regular 10:10 challenge, the people who do it are always amazed at how much they can get done in ten minutes.

Get your to-do list and pick three things, using their order of importance and including any task you have been avoiding. Take the thing you want to do least and make it your first ten-minute task. Think how great you are going to feel once it's done.

There will be some tasks that take more than ten minutes, so break those larger tasks down. If you need five concentrated ten-minute sessions, you can still focus and get things done far more quickly than you have done before.

Timed tasks will give you more time. Short bursts of focused work without interruptions are of far more value than hours of procrastination and avoidance. Give it a go right now.

The structure of your business

The structure of your business controls its function. If you have shaky foundations, no matter how hard you try, things will be difficult. Think about it. If you are in control of the daily pattern of your business, ensuring you take tons of effective action, it will function as you want it to.

As an osteopath, I was taught a key principle: structure governs function when we're talking about the ability of the body to perform well. Put simply, an osteopath's intent is to work on the body's structure to allow optimum function to occur. Your business is no different. You put in the work and your business will flourish. If you lack structure, persistency and consistency, you will constantly be struggling in your business.

CHALLENGE – STRUCTURE YOUR BUSINESS

The first thing you need to do is to structure your working week. You need time to work on your business and in your business, and time off from your business. What days will you see clients? What time will you set aside each week to work on your business? Map out your week.

Please don't tell me you don't have enough time. To be really effective, you need to manage your time, and if you look carefully at your twenty-four hours, you will likely see that you are wasting a lot of it. We all have the same twenty-four hours in a day, but some people – usually those with the busiest of lives – get the most done in that time. Others make excuses for lack of time and why they can't make more of what they have.

Make sure you are not the person who is blaming your children, elderly parents, family, health issues etc. If you have a lot on your plate, then you are the only person who can structure your time.

How can you take really effective action if you are struggling to manage the time you have? If you are busy, and I mean honestly busy, you need to make the most of your hours. I wrote this book between 5 and 6 am every day for six weeks. I needed to make more time for myself, and that was the perfect way to structure some extra hours into my busy day.

You don't have to be an early bird to get success, but if you look at many of the most successful people in this world, you will find they are up early, making the most of their day. They report feeling more energised, creative and able to deal with whatever the day throws at them as a result. I totally agree as that is how I feel when I'm up and taking action early in the day. For me, rising early is like my own secret extra time. The house is silent, the emails are not yet entering my inbox and social media is pretty quiet. The distractions are low, so my productivity and creativity go through the roof.

When you rise early, it is good to have a few rules in place. I never snooze; once I'm awake, I roll over, get up and pull on some comfortable loose-fitting clothes or my gym kit. I never move fast; I just slowly ease myself into my day. Usually it's a time to clear up a few bits in my kitchen and become the dishwasher fairy, which is a great way to start the day. No thought needed, just time to get my body moving and my mind alert.

Next, depending on the day, I either do a workout or I get working on my to-do list. Often after training, I will sit down and write articles and blogs. Training is a great time for me to get ideas, and the early hours are when I tend to be at my most creative. Often I have completed my exercise routine, showered and created some worthwhile content before 7.30 am. It is a wonderful feeling, so I would urge you not to be put off by early starts. If you are up past midnight every night, then it's going to be hard to get up at 5 am, but you can retrain your circadian rhythm. Try a week of going to bed at 11 pm instead, then try 10.30 pm. Gradually your body will readjust.

Some people may feel they get their best work done late at night, but I think early mornings are even more effective if you can retrain yourself. In the morning, you're at the start of a new day. Working late can mean that you're coming off the back of a hard and tiring day, and that is not conducive to doing your best work. It's also likely that later on in the day, you will find excuses for not doing your planned work. It is not my place to tell you to become an early riser, but I will encourage you to try it for a few weeks. It will be a revelation to you once your body switches its time clock, and getting work/exercise done early frees the rest of the day for doing what you love.

If you want to take effective action, it's time to give this a try. You are likely to be amazed at how much work you can get done in a short space of time.

Conclusion

Marketing your business to get the success you dream of is not just a case of knowing the correct methods to use. Of course, you need to know those methods, but you also need to take a journey through each of my five Commit to Achieve principles to ensure you take effective action consistently and persistently.

You really can achieve anything when you learn to commit. If you make sure you follow each principle, taking effective action will become an easy and natural thing to do. Don't be tempted to skip any one of the Commit to Achieve principles; I have set them up as a solid structure for you to follow to get the results you want with the least amount of anxiety and stress, so don't underestimate the power of each one. Use them as your own template for success.

Here is a quick reminder of the five Commit to Achieve principles.

Care of self. Make sure you are looking after yourself as self-care is an essential part of your business success. It may seem like an area that you can overlook, but trust me, if you feel fit and well, your business will flourish. When you are at your healthiest, you will perform at your best. You will get things done with less fuss and stress, your positivity will soar, and you will wonder why you didn't address this sooner.

Know your why. Know why you do what you do and set goals and targets to achieve what you want. Make your why strong enough to push you forward. Remember your why is likely to change over the life of your business, so keep revisiting your reasons. Never give up on building the business you want. Never let others tell you how your business should be and always aim high.

Release your limiting beliefs. Smash those limiting beliefs before they put a stop to your action taking. Don't underestimate the power of imposter syndrome or lack of confidence to stop you in your tracks; understand that you are in control of how you see the world around you. Watch out for the curveballs that life will inevitably throw at you, pick them up and throw them right back – hard.

Understand how. This principle covers marketing methods that don't involve heavy sales, but instead incorporate your natural empathetic and supportive nature to help those who may need your help. Now you understand the marketing methods that you can use for your business without feeling sleazy, you will see more ideal clients and income in your business as a result.

Take effective action. Now you are ready to take action and really be effective. No more being busy while still not making the right impact on your business. With structure in your business and timed tasks to get your to-do list done, you can manage your time effectively, ensuring you enjoy what you do and take time off while still keeping all the things you need to get done under control.

Does all that sound good? Yes, it does! It's time to stop talking about it, get off your butt and get started, and remember all the advice in this book is for the life of your business. Time to be persistent and consistent.

Go!

Acknowledgements

Well, who would have thought that me – the girl who struggled at school to write a grammatically correct sentence – would ever be writing acknowledgements for my own book. It's exciting and it is also necessary, as I am fully aware that without the support of those around me this would not have happened.

I am a force of nature and a whirlwind at times and the first people I need to thank are my family. My partner and my children put up with my ramblings and the constant talking about the book. Their support in everything I do is unrelenting and I am thankful to them all for believing in me and what I do.

Sue Ford, one of my close friends and assistant coach on my UK retreats, was there to encourage me, look at drafts, trawl through the mass of words and help me rationalise things. She never once complained. Coffee was our go-to support during this time.

Debbie Frost, my practice manager and close friend, must also get a thanks for being the backbone (excuse the pun) of my clinic, Fine Fettle. Without Debbie working alongside me I would be unable to run two businesses so successfully. Everyone needs a Debbie as a practice manager and best friend! We started as friends and teammates during our years of playing National League volleyball together back in our twenties and that background of team spirit and competitiveness has served us both well.

I want to publicly thank Freda Bussey, founder of the Ashcombe Volleyball Club, for being the first person to see something in me.

I also want to thank Melanie Coutinho, the principal of my college in my final year and another key person in my journey of change. She always believed in me, pushing me beyond my own expectations and limiting beliefs and spurring me on to lecture internationally, and become part of the osteopathic management team and vice principal of a new osteopathic course in Dublin. Today I am proud to count Melanie as one of my closest and most trusted friends. I would literally do anything for her, and I know she would do the same for me.

Over the last three years I have been fortunate to have been mentored by some awesome coaches and without their help, ideas and belief this book would never have been written. Thanks must go to Shaa Wasmund and Dax Moy. They both were instrumental in showing me I had more to give and, with their support and my work and perseverance, they showed me anything was possible. Shaa explained how I could structure my mentoring business and how to think bigger. Dax has to be thanked for being one of the few people brave enough to tell me to stop my drama and to reassure me it was OK to run my business my own way. Both have been instrumental in me getting to this point, and I am proud to thank them publicly here.

Huge thanks must go to my awesome team of beta readers who were sent my book in its very early stages to plough through my version of English grammar and find the essence of this book in its infancy. Huge thanks to Martin File, Claire Baker, Stephanie Bourner, Sue Ford, and Mel Coutinho for their awesome feedback and support. Their expertise was vital to make sure this book was sending out the right message and that it would help therapists get more from their businesses.

Lastly, a huge shout out to my therapy business support group, Helen's Business Club, who have been there throughout this process, watching, listening and cheering me on. They are my biggest supporters, as

I am to them. Special thanks to one member, Martin File, who came up with the awesome title for this book. I am very proud of the group and the support they give to each other and that they have shown to me in this process.

The Author

Helen Bullen BSc (Hons) Osteopathic Medicine is a business mentor, osteopath, lecturer and owner of Fine Fettle Multi-healthcare, a large multi-healthcare centre. She runs an online membership group called Helen's Business Club that helps therapists build their clinics. She also runs business retreats in the UK and Thailand as well as one-day business training events.

Helen has fourteen years of experience teaching osteopaths, sports therapists and sports masseurs. Her teaching work has included the roles of senior tutor, module leader and MSc co-ordinator at the

Surrey Institute of Osteopathic Medicine, and at the Irish College of Osteopaths in Dublin where she was the vice principal for three years. She has also taught sports and remedial massage to students at the Raworth College, Dorking; The Paragon College in Leatherhead; The London School of Health and Beauty; and the RAF, Navy and Army PT instructors at Headley Court in Leatherhead. She has lectured internationally to osteopathic and physiotherapy students in Italy. Helen worked for Wales University as an external examiner for osteopathic schools in Ghent, Belgium and Milan and has been a subject expert for Swansea University for an Osteopathic Course in Turin.

Over the years Helen has won multiple awards for both her clinic and her business acumen. For six years she sat on the Investigating Committee for her governing body, the General Osteopathic Council.

Helen's experience of building a clinic from scratch means she has first-hand experience of working as a therapist. She has undertaken further business management training to increase her knowledge and understanding of modern-day marketing. Helen is known for her honest and straight-talking style of mentoring combined with empathy and understanding. 'Kindly blunt' and 'kick-butt motivator' are common ways to describe her.

You can contact Helen on:

■ www.facebook.com/hbullen

Commit to Achieve Facebook group: www.facebook.com/groups/COMMITtoACHIEVE

⊙ helenbullenuk

Printed in Great Britain
by Amazon